Table of Contents

A. Complete Fill in the Blanks Business Plan Template

It is recommended that you download the MS Word Doc version of this template to easily edit and modify it to meet your own specific needs (compatible with most word processors).

The download link is presented at the end of the book; see the first item in the "Special Free Bonuses" section.

Business Plan Table of Contents

Table of Contents

1.0 Executive Summary

Introduction

[Company Name] is two bed & breakfast houses located in the heart of Napa Valley. The company operates from [Address, City, State ZIP]. Each historical house is built in the late 19th century, with five charmingly decorated rooms geared to provide luxurious hospitality at its finest.

- ***The 1872 Victorian Style Ambrose Bierce House***
- ***The Shady Oaks Country Inn on 2 acres land***

The Market

The Napa Valley is one of California's number one vacation destination locations. A statistical report shows that 2.75 million overnight trips were made to this area with bed and breakfast reflecting an annual revenue income of $40 million. 60.9% of travelers are over the age of 45 with an average income of over $100,000 per year. The total economic impact of visitors to Napa County was $1.3 billion in 2005.

The Management Team

[Name], a husband and wife team has managed these two Inns for over twenty-four years showing a steady income growth over the years. Their expertise in hospitality totals over 60 years combined and is a direct reflection of their word to mouth marketing strategy. Community leadership and local annual donations are just a few aspects [Name] and [Name] pride themselves with. Local wineries will recommend the Inns to their customers which almost always lead to repeat visitors to St. Helena.

The Company

With ten rooms over two properties, the owners have a solid income stream and a 10% market share to this area. Adding additional marketing will draw new and existing customers for this tourist attraction. Renovating, remodeling, and adding rooms will help local vendors with their business.

[Company Name]is committed to participate in reviving the economy and return the sales to the heart of the Napa Valley. These opportunities will ensure a strong competitive edge to other bed and breakfasts and at the same time implement a long-term revenue stream.

The Request

An immediate grant in the amount of **$250,000** will allow to

Increase Marketing Efforts - $60,000

Renovate and upgrade existing rooms - $119,000

Add two rooms - $71,000

A second grant one year later in the amount of **$100,000** would allow to add three more rooms - $100,000

This capital injection will create jobs, labor work, and additional reservation count. With an average annual capacity of 43% - 47%, the added rooms would generate a new revenue stream of an additional 33% to the Inns. Projecting only 30% of capacity for the FY 2011 and 2012 would yield an additional income of **$127,567**. As the highlights reflect, sales could reach over $500,000 by year three from receipt of capital.

This additional income and the projected gross profits will support the overall efforts in hiring a total of five more employees over the next three years.

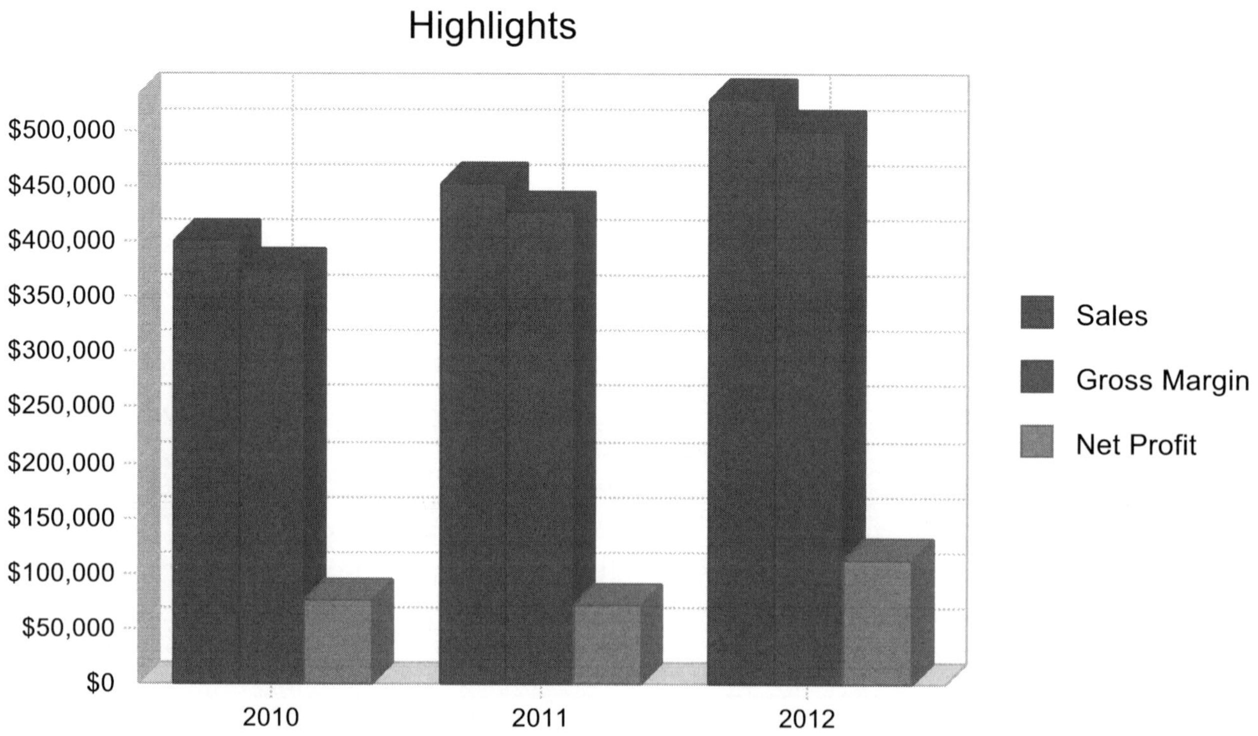

1.1 Objectives

The [Company Name]s' concept for this business plan is to obtain an immediate capital injection in the amount of $250,000 to address the following areas needed for the Inns and a second injection of $100,000 one year thereafter to add three additional rooms.

Realizing these objectives will boost the revenue streams, add jobs to the community, and inject labor jobs for a period of three years for the renovation, remodeling, and addition projects.

- **Marketing - $60,000**

    - Paid search engine listing to reach a higher presence on the internet "hit" rate
    - Upgrade websites
    - Produce direct mailers to existing and new customers
    - Create e-blast e-mail advertisements

- Produce brochures and pamphlets for local advertisement

- **Remodel and Upgrade existing rooms - $119,000**

    - Replace carpets
    - Upgrade bathrooms and tubs (include conversion of two tubs into jetted tubs)
    - Purchase furniture and beds
    - Interior and exterior painting at Shady Oaks Country Inn
    - Add fireplaces to five rooms
    - Upgrade flooring to increase AAA rating

- **Expansion of two rooms at Ambrose Bierce House - $71,000**

    - Add two rooms

- **Future Expansion of three additional rooms at Shady Oaks Country Inn - $100,000**

a. Add thee rooms

1.2 Mission

The [Company Name]s' mission is to provide luxurious and hospitable lodging at an affordable price. The goal is to give guests a wonderful Bed and breakfast experience and assist them in their Napa Valley vacation.

1.3 Keys to Success

[Company Name]keys to success for the Napa Valley bed and breakfast Inns are:

- The great location of the Inns with access to the vineyards and wine train
- Local presence of over 24 years in business
- Highly recommended by local winery owners
- Proven track record of successful profit making operation over the past 24 years
- Community leadership and support
- Excellent service with "personal touch" hospitality

2.0 Company Summary

The target market is adult couples between ages 24 and 75 years visiting the Napa Valley as well as visitors arriving in St. Helena without reservations.

[Company Name]s LLC operates two bed and breakfasts in the heart of Napa Valley in St. Helena, California which are:

[Company Name]

[Company Name]

2.1 Company Ownership

[Company Name]s is a Limited Liability Corporation operated by its original owners:

[Name]

Both, [Name] and [Name] have been in the hospitality industry for more than 30 years each.

2.2 Company History

[Company Name]s LLC was formed in **[Date]**. [Name] have been operating these two facilities from the Napa Valley vacation destination infancy, contributing a tremendous amount of success with regards to the lodging and hospitality support. This success is reflected by the local recommendations made by vineyard owners who suggest the Inns for their overnight stay.

While the beautiful vineyards offer one of California's finest wines, it is the Inns unprecedented personal service and their charmingly decorated rooms that create the memorable experience for visitors to return and new ones to choose the Inns.

In the last 10 years, the Napa Valley wine country also attracted a more high-end wealthier clientele, making the Napa Valley a number one tourist attraction in California. As a result of this attraction, in the past five years, the numbers of available rooms have risen.

The economic challenges of the recent 18 months have placed a financial burden on the Inns that creates a challenge for competition. The solutions represented in this Business Plan are geared towards the reviving aspects of the visitor attraction, keeping up with the new marketing and advertising technology, and to upgrade, remodel, and add more rooms to the Inns. Both of the Inns are historical buildings constructed in the late nineteenth century and require a great deal of upkeep.

Table: Past Performance

Past Performance			
	2007	**2008**	**2009**
Sales	$402,926	$475,746	$341,965
Gross Margin	$0	$0	$0
Gross Margin %	0.00%	0.00%	0.00%
Operating Expenses	$397,987	$389,731	$347,229
Balance Sheet			
	2007	2008	2009
Current Assets			
Cash	$19,365	$18,000	$21,000
Other Current	$225,000	$271,000	$247,000

Assets			
Total Current Assets	$244,365	$289,000	$268,000
Long-term Assets			
Long-term Assets	$1,237,000	$1,734,000	$1,990,000
Accumulated Depreciation	$0	$0	$0
Total Long-term Assets	$1,237,000	$1,734,000	$1,990,000
Total Assets	$1,481,365	$2,023,000	$2,258,000
Current Liabilities			
Accounts Payable	$36,900	$2,600	$5,900
Current Borrowing			
Other Current Liabilities (interest free)	$0	$0	$0
Total Current Liabilities	$36,900	$2,600	$5,900
Long-term Liabilities	$684,000	$674,000	$664,000
Total Liabilities	$720,900	$676,600	$669,900
Paid-in Capital	$0	$0	$0
Retained Earnings	$760,465	$1,346,400	$1,588,100

Earnings	$0	$0	$0
Total Capital	$760,465	$1,346,400	$1,588,100
Total Capital and Liabilities	$1,481,365	$2,023,000	$2,258,000
Other Inputs			
Payment Days	0	0	0

Chart: Past Performance

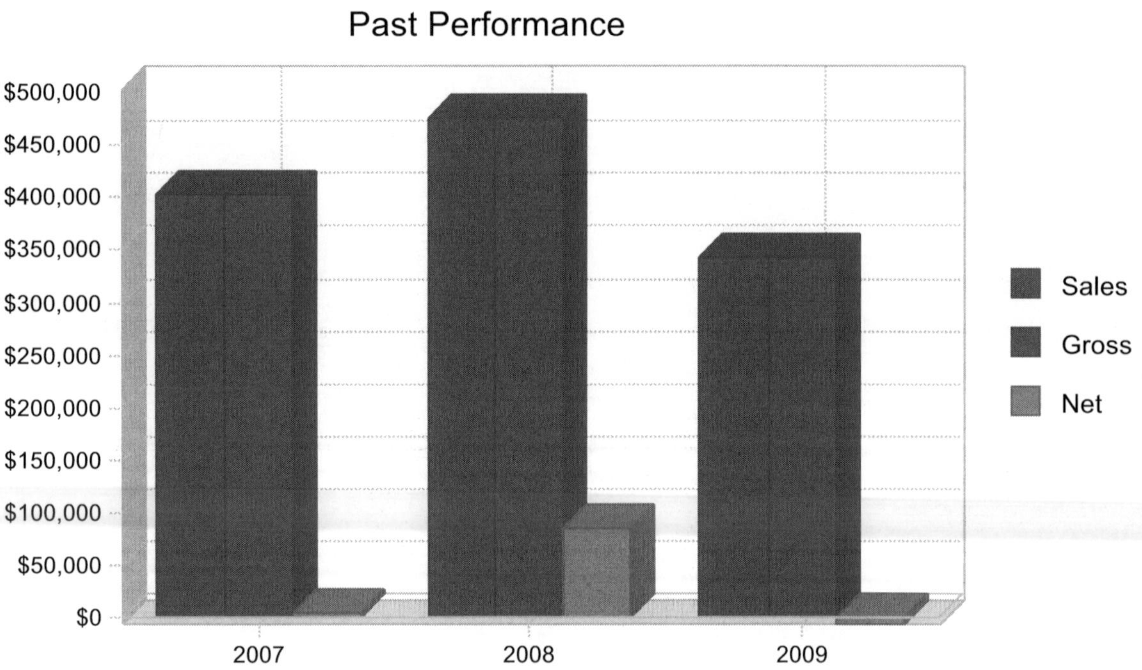

3.0 Services

Both bed and breakfast properties offer lodging in a luxurious and intimate setting. The owners offer special attention to their guests, a tranquilizing ambiance, and a relaxing atmosphere in the heart of the Napa Valley.

- **The 1872 Romantic Victorian Style - Ambrose Bierce House B&B - average room/suite rate of $227.00/night**
    - 5 Rooms Total

- **The Shady Oaks Country Inn on two acres - average room/suite rate of $249.00/night**
    - 5 Rooms Total

Both Inns offer amenities such as:

- Ambrose Bierce House B&B: Location is in walking distance to the wine train

    - Shady Oaks Country Inn: Location is on two acres amidst the vineyards

Both Inns offer rooms available with:

- Jacuzzi Tubs
- Fireplaces (in room)
- Satellite TV / Internet Access
- Air Conditioning
- Balcony / Deck
- Parlor

Specialty amenities include:

- The famous Champagne Breakfast
- Wine and cheese every evening

4.0 Market Analysis Summary

Napa Valley and its Tourism

A recent study named "Napa County Visitor Profile Study & Napa County Economic Impact Study" published in March 2006 revealed very important tourism and economical statistics regarding the impact tourism has on Napa Valley. Below are key findings that directly impact the marketing analysis for the bed and breakfast properties.

How much does a Visitor spent?

Visitors who did not stay overnight within Napa County spent an average of $146 per-day, **while overnight visitors spent $233 per-day**. Average total Daily Spending of both categories is $197.Tourism in Napa County generates over $1.3 Billion in economic impact annually.

The visitor serving industry is the second largest sector of Napa County's economy. Every 24 hours, guests of The Napa Valley spend approximately $4 million in local businesses, with Napa visitors contributing about $176 million to the revenue of commercial hotels in Napa County. **Bed and breakfasts received another $40 million of their revenue from visitors.** Tax revenue generated by tourism spending is **$125 million annually**.

In addition to the well known winery attraction, the Napa Valley has many other great activities that draw tourists to stay additional days. Some of the activities include:

- California Wine purchase and vineyard visits
- Fine Dining
- Art
- Hot Air Ballooning and Bicycling
- Golf
- Casinos
- Site Seeing Tours
- Spas / Massage
- Shopping
- Museum and Live Performances and Tours

4.1 Market Segmentation

Visitor Age Profile

The largest age group of respondents in the annual sample was between **35 and 44 years.** They made up **21%.** The age composition of all visitors showed a more senior picture, with the **45-54** age groups making up **23%** of all visitors represented by the total annual sample. Respondents between **35 and 54 years** of age (three age groups combined) made up close to **50%** of the annual total sample. Those at the age of **45 and above** accounted for **60.9%** of all visitors.

Visitor Income Profile

- $100,000 and over = 57.6%
- $150,000 and over = 26.6%
- $50,000 to $99,000 = 30.1%

Visitors Education Profile

- Professional and Technical = 30.2%
- Managers and Executives = 23.7%
- From the above sample about 73.5% hold a bachelor's to doctorate degree
- and 32.1% hold a master's and doctorate degree

How many visitors stay at a bed and breakfast annually?

According to the above statistics, approximately **171,673 visitors** utilized a **Bed and breakfast** for their lodging needs.

How likely are the Visitors to return to the Napa Valley and when?

This question is extremely important to [Company Name]operation as it directly impacts their repetitive customer base. The Inns pride themselves with service that is worth coming back for. Therefore, we opted to illuminate this aspect in the Market Analysis. The findings are:

Napa Valley's travel market can be considered as highly loyal. The proportion of all guests who expressed either **"very likely" or "likely" to return to the area** for future visits was nearly **90.1%**.

This strongly suggests that the more often they visit the area and the more they know about it, the more likely they are to return. Among those who expressed a likelihood of future visits, **22.1%** would come back within **three months**; another **34.7%** between **four months and one year**.

Table: Market Analysis

Market Analysis					
		2010	2011	2012	
Potential Customers	Growth				CAGR
Age Group 35-44 (21%)	3%	36,052	37,134	38,248	3.00%
Age Group 45-54 (23%)	3%	39,485	40,670	41,890	3.00%
Age Group 45+ (60.8%)	3%	104,375	107,506	110,731	3.00%

Total	3.00%	179,912	185,310	190,869	3.00%

Chart: Market Analysis

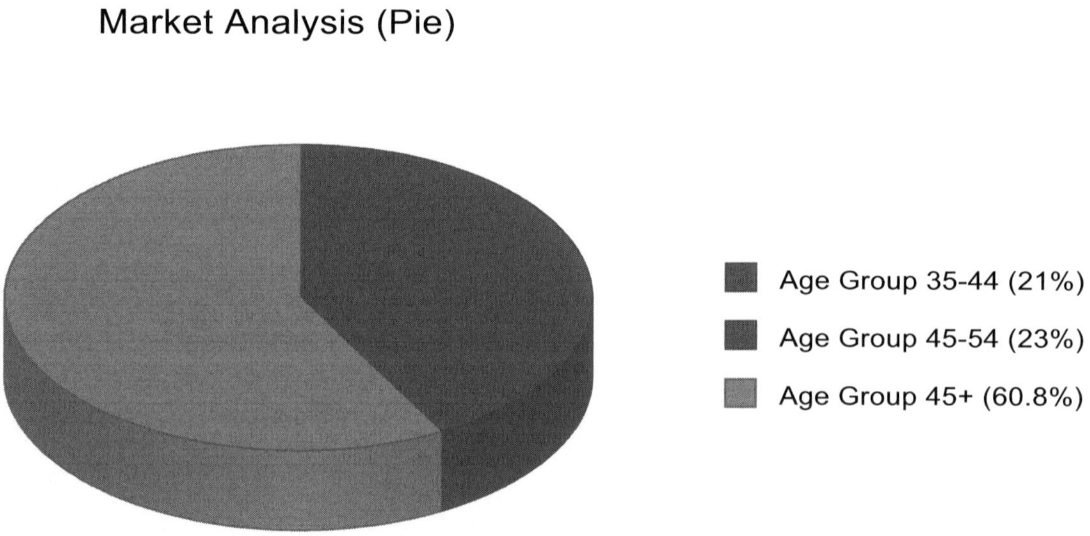

4.2 Target Market Segment Strategy

The Inns targeted market groups are couples ranging from age 24 to 75 years of age seeking to visit the Napa Valley. The major focus group which is also the highest percentage of visitors to this area would be those of age 45 and over making up over 60% of the total visitors to the Napa Valley. The secondary group classification would be the income level of $100,000 and above, making up about 86.2% of visitors.

4.3 Service Business Analysis

The [Company Name]s offer bed and breakfast hospitality accommodations as well as some food service for their guests. The Shady Oaks Country Inn and The Ambrose Bierce House B&B each have five distinctively and individually decorated rooms for rent. Aside from the room, the Inns offer breakfast and wine & cheese in the evening.

4.3.1 Competition and Buying Patterns

Both of the Inns are competitively prices at an average price of $245.00/night. The intimate atmosphere which is created by the historical properties is an important aspect that new buildings can not compete with. Additionally, the Owners have a proven track record of returning guests based on the customer service, the rooms, and the personal attention they provide.

The Inns' greatest assets are the location of the Inns and the owner's long time community relationships with the town and county. This presence and involvement from the beginning of this tourist attraction are all added values that set the Inns apart from newly introduced bed and breakfast properties in the Napa Valley. The Shady Oaks Country Inn is one of only three bed and breakfast location in this immediate area.

5.0 Strategy and Implementation Summary

Tourists visiting the Napa Valley expect to vacation amidst the vineyards, restaurants, and shops in an atmosphere that "takes them back in time". Equipped with the amenities a modern traveler needs today, the owners have maintained this distinct "time capsule" ambiance through their perfectly situated 19th century bed and breakfasts. The goals of the Inn are two-sided; preserving these revenue making buildings and continue to provide exceptional memories to tourists visiting the beautiful enchanted Napa Valley.

5.1 SWOT Analysis

The [Company Name]s **strengths** are the locations, the 19th century historical buildings, and their original owners for over twenty-four years of operations are their major assets. Stemming from these strengths is a repetitive customer base through positive word of mouth recommendations from local winery owners, restaurants, and shops. The historical buildings, a major marketing asset, also create a **weakness** in regards to the costs associated with the maintenance and upkeep. Coupled with the economic challenges, a capital injection would yield a positive solution to upgrade and remodel these Inns while creating equity on the balance sheet.

These upgrades also present an **opportunity** for the Inns to create a competitive edge driven by added visibility on the internet to reach new customer who, no doubt, will become repeat guests. The noted weaknesses are ultimate the **threats** to the Inns which can be eliminated by implementing these opportunities.

5.1.1 Strengths

Great Locations: Both Inns are perfectly situated to accommodate two major groups of visitors

- Guest who wish to walk to restaurants and downtown shopping. Ambrose Bierce House is located in walking distance to the wine train.
- Or Guests who wish to be on the country side among the vineyards on a two acre land.

Experience & Presence: The original owners of twenty-four years also have over thirty years of experience in the hospitality industry. Coupled with the knowledge, the owners have built a tremendous amount of reputation, trust, and community support over the years. These owners have operated longer than any other Innkeepers in this area.

Napa Valley Community Involvement: From the start of operating the Inns, both [Name] have been active members of the St. Helena Chamber of Commerce and have been on the board of the Napa Valley Visitors and Convention Bureau. Giving back to the community is a philosophy that comes naturally. **Each year donations of fifteen room nights are made available to benefit the local community services such as the St. Helena Rotary and the local school scholarship fund.**

5.1.2 Weaknesses

- The needed cash flow from profits is a result of the recent economic challenges. The Inns are historical buildings and need constant upkeep.
- Having to lay off four employees who are needed to maintain the Inns and to service the guests.
- The need for more internet presence through paid search engine tools to gain a higher reservation "hit rate".
-

5.1.3 Opportunities

- Travelers seeking reservations online will allow for the needed visibility to attract guests from all regions of the United States and world wide.
- The Napa Valley, for the past five years, has been the number one destination point in California. Preparing for the

economical recovery, the owners will utilize the time to remodel and upgrade the Inns.

- Hiring five employees will create the needed labor force to assist with guest services
- Placing ads in magazines specifically for the San Francisco bay area
- Maintain communication with the existing customers on a regular basis (4 times a year)
- Attracting those guests with no reservation by local advertisement
- Adding five rooms over a period of three years will generate a higher revenue stream

5.1.4 Threats

- Lack of funding to maintain, remodel, and upgrade the historical buildings
- Low visibility on the internet to reach new guests
- Limited funds to maintain communications with repeat customers
- Unable to re-hire the needed employees
- Maintaining the Inns' competitive edge from emerging local competitors

5.2 Competitive Edge

The tangible competitive edge the Inns have over other lodging facilities are easily identified as:

- The owners who have diligently serviced the hospitality needs of thousands of guests for the past 24 years
- The 19th. century historic buildings bring the bed and breakfast to live with each room idyllically decorated

- Both bed and breakfast are perfectly situated in the heart of Napa Valley
- Ambrose Bierce House B&B was bought at a time when prices were low
- Having a twenty year lease on Shady Oaks Country Inn - one of only three Inns available in the area

5.3 Marketing Strategy

Internet Search Engine Upgrade:

Upgrade the URL links to be added to paid search engine return results. Add more keywords, and maintain service to stay on the top 10 hit return list when users search for Napa Valley accommodations.

Direct Print Mailers & E-Mail:

Sent out e-mails and postcard mailers of updates from the bed and breakfast highlights, inform about upcoming events, and announce annual festivals to the existing customer base. Mailers should be sent at least four times a year. Addresses are available through the reservation system by zip code, status, and other criteria.

Local Print Advertising:

Advertise locally for those travelers without any reservations. Main focus is directed at winery, restaurants and shops in the Napa Valley. Maps of winery, local magazines, and free brochures are available for advertising.

5.4 Sales Strategy

The [Company Name]s have fully functioning websites with reservation tools in place for each location. Currently, 72% of their reservations are made online.

- Paid search engine tool to increase internet presence
- Update website with flash player, new high graphic pictures, and interactive reservation tools
- Add more direct mailers and e-mail campaigners for existing customers
- Distribute more brochures and pamphlets at local places such as the winery, restaurants, and shops

5.4.1 Sales Forecast

The table below outlines the sales projections for the next three years (including 2010 current) based on both Inns with a total of 10 rooms combined. The direct costs associated with the sales are also combined and reflect an approximate 3% margin for the credit card merchant fee, a 6% margin for the Food and Beverages, and a 2% margin for Other Supplies and Linen from the annual Gross Sales amount.

In FY2010 sales are forecasted to include the marketing impact for the added visibility on paid search engines and a total of a 10 room capacity at 47% or $400,000 per year. FY-2011 sales include two additional rooms respectively an added revenue stream of $170,090, a 30% capacity of the added rooms would generate additional sales of $51,027 per year thus impacting the overall sales to $452,000 at a 44% capacity level.

In FY-2012 the added three rooms would generate even more revenues to the overall sales in the amount of approximately $255,135 per year. A 30% capacity of the added three rooms would generate additional sales in the amount of approximately $76,540 per year thus impacting the overall sales to $527,541 at a 41% capacity level.

Renovating, upgrading, and adding the five rooms over a period of three years will proof beneficial to the overall revenue stream to the Inns.

The current 100% revenues are reflective of about 3,650 reservations with a maximum income of $850,450. By the end of year three this revenue stream will be at 5,475 reservation opportunities with an increased revenue opportunity of $1,276,675.

A $350,000 grant capital injection would yield 27% in new revenue opportunities.

Table: Sales Forecast

Sales Forecast			
	2010	2011	2012
Sales			
Ambrose Bierce House B&B	$148,500	$167,805	$195,325
Shady Oaks Country Inn	$251,500	$284,195	$332,224
	$0	$0	$0
Total Sales	$400,000	$452,000	$527,549
Direct Cost of Sales	2010	2011	2012
Credit Card Merchant Fee	$6,600	$6,732	$6,867
Food and Beverage	$14,400	$14,688	$14,982
Other Supplies and Linen	$4,800	$4,896	$4,994
Subtotal Direct Cost of Sales	$25,800	$26,316	$26,842

Chart: Sales Monthly

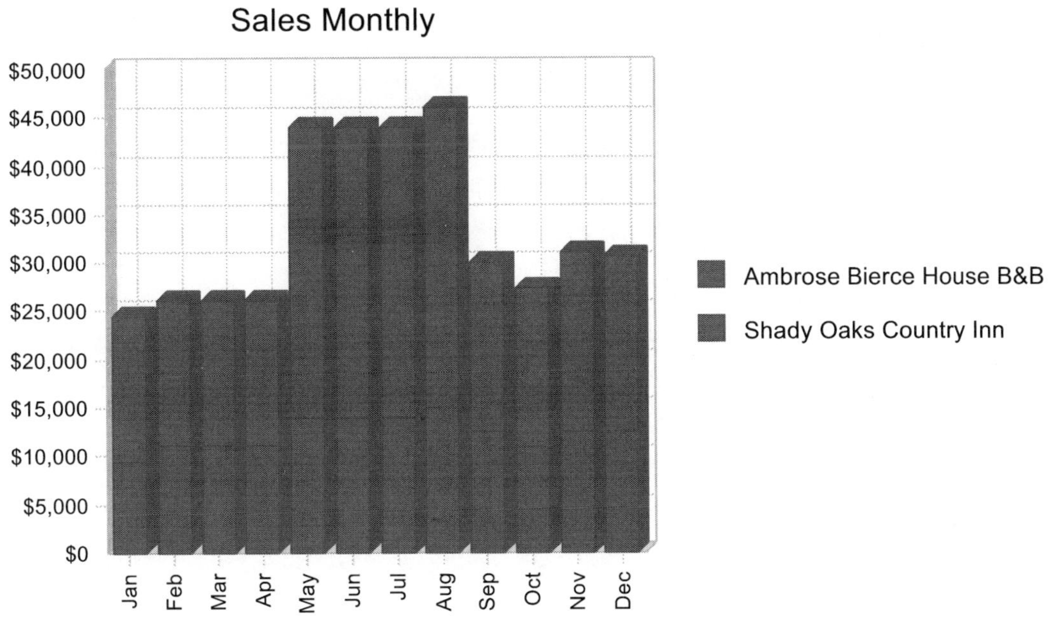

Chart: Sales by Year

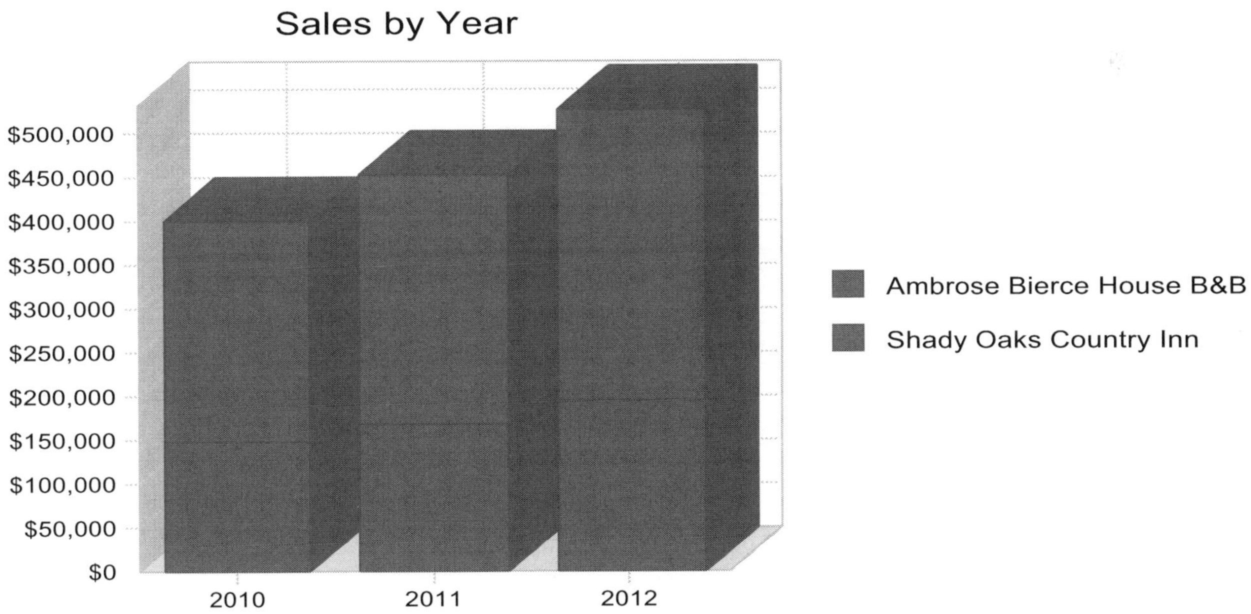

5.5 Milestones

The following table lists important milestone dates and budget amounts. Upon receipt of the anticipated capital injection of $250,000, the internet search engine development can start immediately.

Print Advertisement is scheduled to be released throughout the year and the remodel/upgrade work is schedule within weeks after receipt of the capital.

Adding two rooms in phase I will increase the added revenue stream for FY-2011 and adding three additional rooms from the second funding of $100,000 will add additional revenue streams for FY-2012.

Table: Milestones

Milestones

Milestone	Start Date	End Date	Budget
Receive capital injection 250K	10/1/2010	11/15/2010	$0
Add Search Engine Tool	10/15/2010	10/15/2011	$42,000
Print Advertisement	10/15/2010	10/15/2011	$18,000
Replace carpet	10/15/2010	11/15/2010	$12,000
Upgrade 6 bathrooms	11/15/2010	12/31/2010	$19,000
Convert 2	11/1/2010	11/30/2010	$8,000

tubs to jetted tubs			
Purchase furniture and beds	1/1/2011	1/15/2011	$28,000
Shady Oaks: Int. & Ext. paint	11/15/2010	11/30/2010	$22,000
Add 5 fireplaces	11/15/2010	1/31/2011	$15,000
Upgrade bathroom flooring	11/15/2010	12/15/2010	$15,000
Add 2 rooms to Ambrose Bierce	11/1/2010	4/1/2010	$71,000
Add 3 rooms to Shady Oaks	10/1/2011	3/1/2012	$100,000
Totals			$350,000

Chart: Milestones

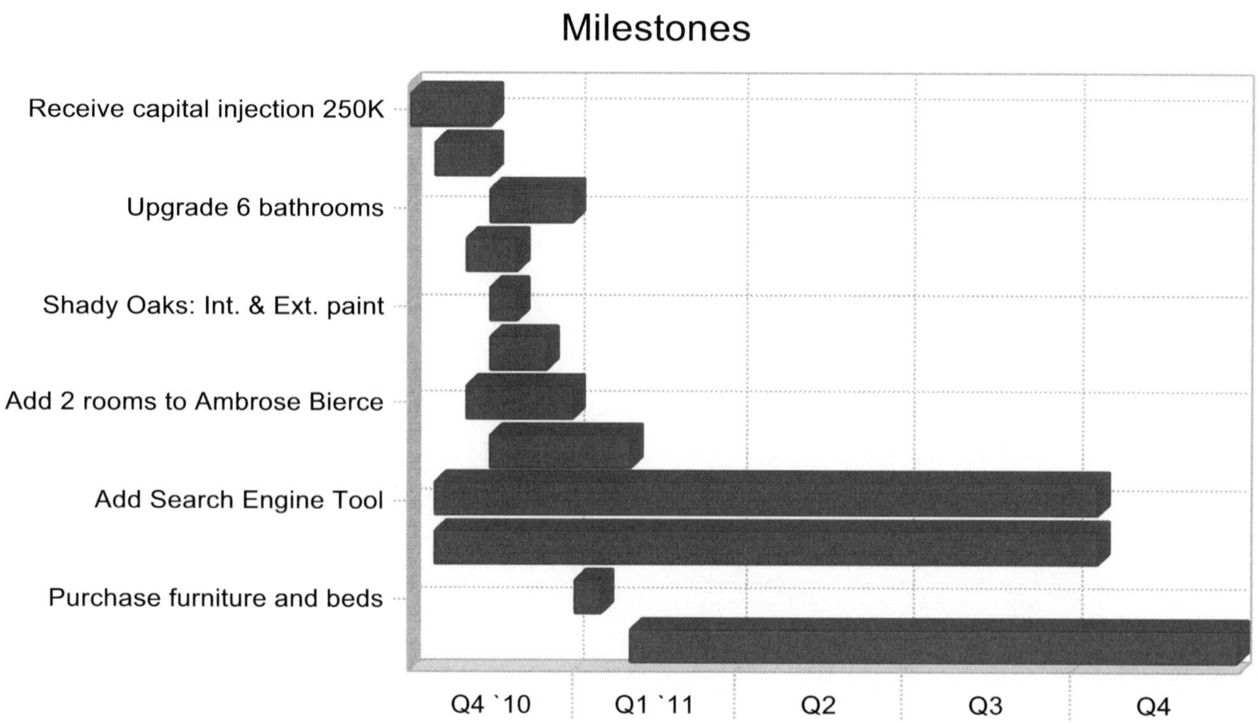

6.0 Management Summary

The Inns are currently operated by the two owners, [Name], a full-time manager, and two hourly housekeeper employees. The company anticipates re-hiring two more employees by November 2010 to assist with the guest services and the remodel and renovation clean up work. One additional employee will be hired by April 2011 when the two rooms are added. Another two employees will be hired by the end of phase II completion of the three rooms in FY-2012.

6.1 Personnel Plan

The Inns will maintain its primary management functions through the current owners.

The manager employee has an annual gross salary of $64,000 and the housekeepers are at a gross hourly rate of $10.00/hour. The current two housekeepers will maintain the current workload until the renovation and remodel begins.

At that time, the Inns plan to hire or re-hire two of the three additional employees to service the facilities and guests. By the end of FY 2012, the Inns anticipate to have eight employees to service the facilities.

Table: Personnel

Personnel Plan			
	2010	2011	2012
Manager	$55,248	$55,248	$55,248
Housekeepers	$30,464	$62,016	$81,600
Total People	5	6	8

Total Payroll	$85,712	$117,264	$136,848

7.0 Financial Plan

The operations of the Inns do not require purchase of inventory and almost all sales are pre-paid or on cash basis, therefore, an increase in sales will not be accompanied by initial cash-flow deficits.

7.1 Important Assumptions

The financial plan depends on several important assumptions such as:

- The capital injections are received
- The paid search engine will attract new customers making online reservations
- The renovation, remodel, and addition will attract new and high-end customers

7.2 Break-even Analysis

The break-even analysis is based on the Inns fixed costs of rent, maintenance, payroll, insurance, and general monthly costs. The monthly revenue break even point for the Inns is at $19,044 with an average percent variable cost of six percent.

Table: Break-even Analysis

Break-even Analysis	
Monthly Revenue Break-even	$19,044
Assumptions:	
Average Percent Variable Cost	6%
Estimated Monthly Fixed Cost	$17,816

Chart: Break-even Analysis

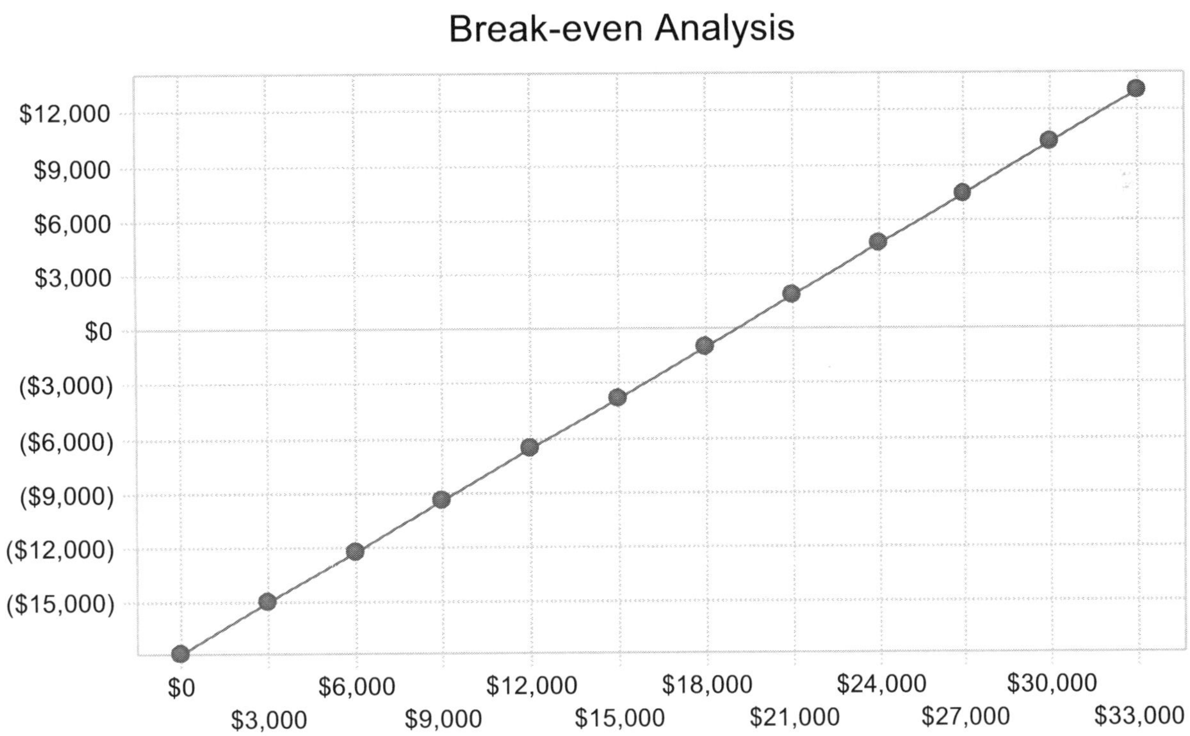

7.3 Projected Profit and Loss

Receiving a capital injection to handle the major marketing costs, renovations, and upgrades will yield a higher profit return for the FY 2010/2011/2012. The anticipated net profits will be used to re-hire and hire six additional employees by FY-2012.

Table: Profit and Loss

Pro Forma Profit and Loss		
	2010	2011
Sales	$400,000	$452,000
Direct Cost of Sales	$25,800	$26,316
Other Costs of Sales	$0	$0
Total Cost of Sales	$25,800	$26,316
Gross Margin	$374,200	$425,684
Gross Margin %	93.55%	94.18%
Expenses		
Payroll	$85,712	$117,264
Rent	$52,500	$52,500

Depreciation	$0	$0
Utilities	$21,000	$21,420
Insurance & Auto Expenses	$15,504	$15,814
Phone/Fax/Internet/Supplies/Equipment	$9,504	$9,694
Payroll Taxes	$2,571	$3,518
Marketing & Advertisement	$12,000	$12,240
Repairs	$15,000	$15,300
Total Operating Expenses	$213,791	$247,750
Profit Before Interest and Taxes	$160,409	$177,934
EBITDA	$160,409	$177,934
Interest Expense	$72,060	$94,767
Taxes Incurred	$13,252	$12,475
Net Profit	$75,096	$70,692
Net Profit/Sales	18.77%	15.64%

Chart: Profit Monthly 2010

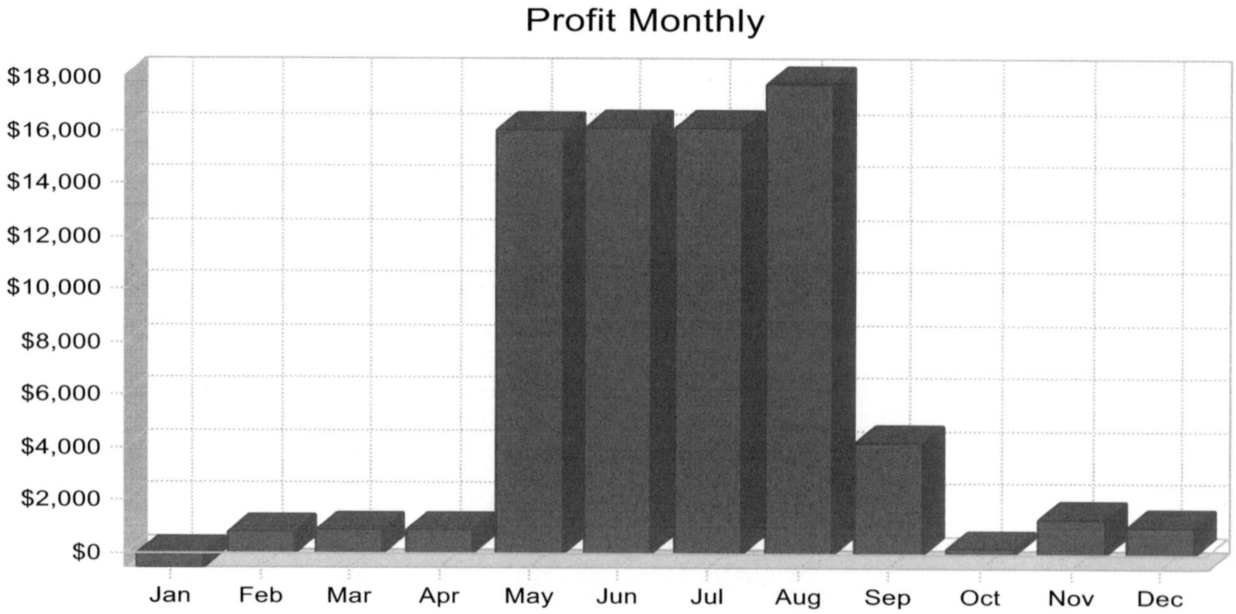

Chart: Profit Yearly

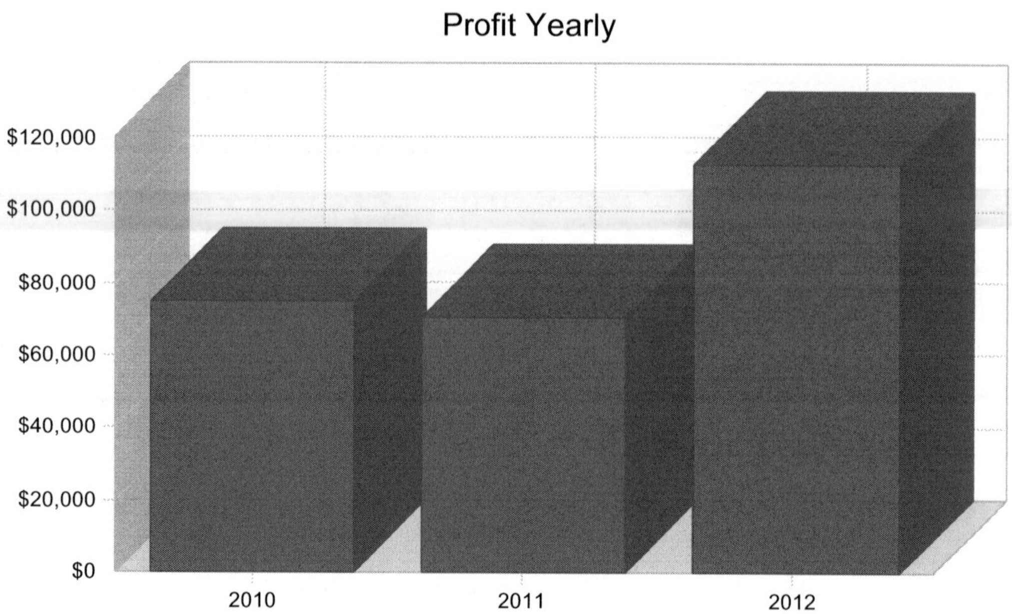

Chart: Gross Margin Monthly

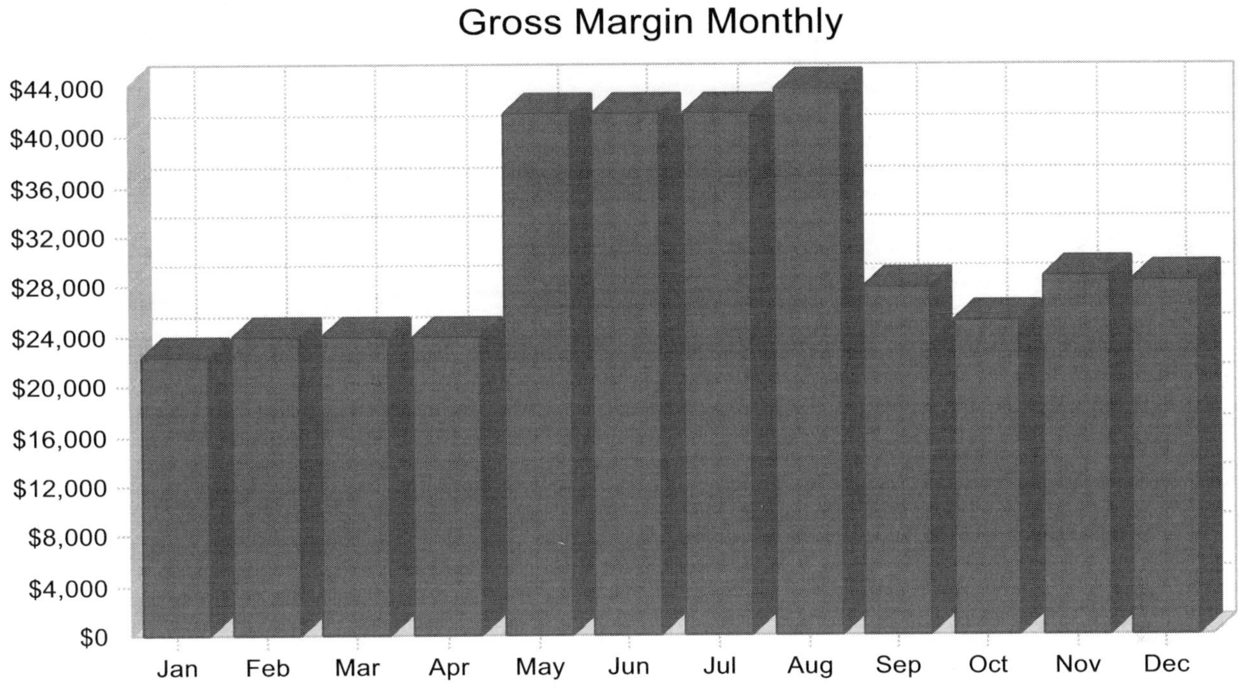

Chart: Gross Margin Yearly

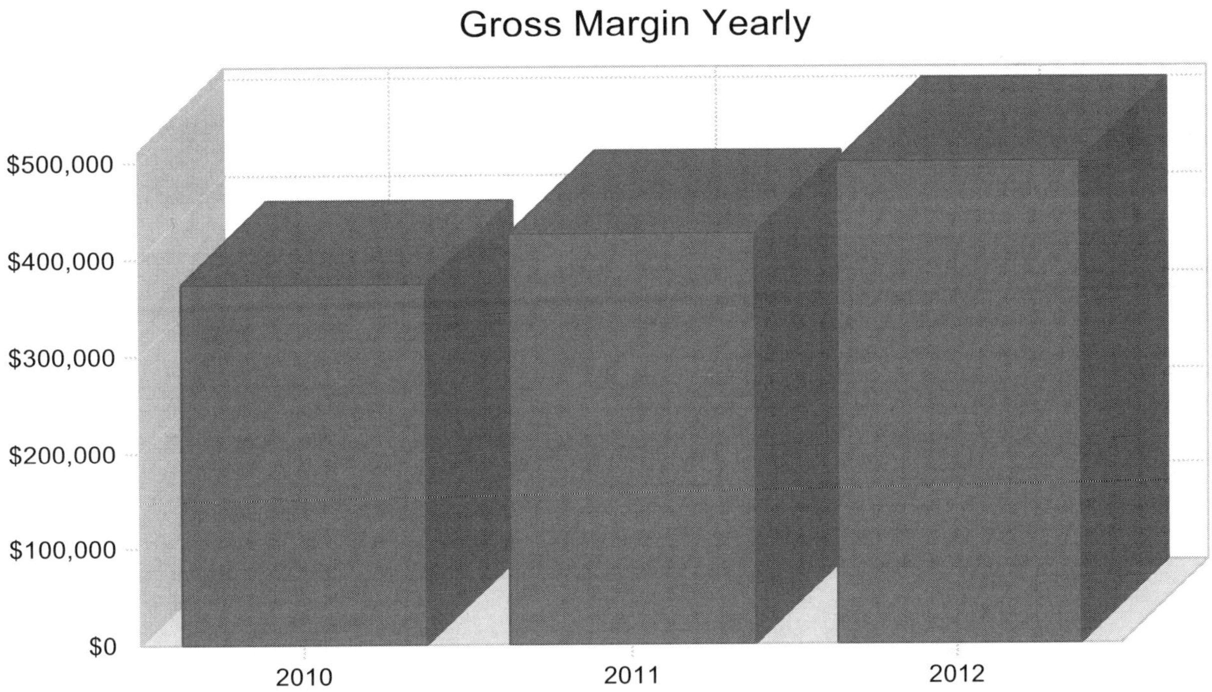

7.4 Projected Cash Flow

According to the projected profit and loss statement, the Inns will make positive cash flow as the capital injection is received towards the end of FY 2010 to address the costs of marketing, renovations, and room additions. Utilizing the capital injection to generate additional revenues and staying competitive in this market will generate sufficient cash flow to support the operations.

Table: Cash Flow

Pro Forma Cash Flow			
	2010	2011	2012
Cash Received			
Cash from Operations			
Cash Sales	$400,000	$452,000	$527,549
Subtotal Cash from Operations	$400,000	$452,000	$527,549
Additional Cash Received			
Sales Tax, VAT, HST/GST Received	$0	$0	$0
New Current Borrowing	$250,000	$100,000	$0
New Other Liabilities (interest-free)	$0	$0	$0
New Long-term Liabilities	$0	$0	$0
Sales of Other Current Assets	$0	$0	$0
Sales of Long-term Assets	$0	$0	$0
New Investment Received	$0	$0	$0

Subtotal Cash Received	$650,000	$552,000	$527,549
Expenditures	2010	2011	2012
Expenditures from Operations			
Cash Spending	$85,712	$117,264	$136,848
Bill Payments	$225,189	$262,246	$276,832
Subtotal Spent on Operations	$310,901	$379,510	$413,680
Additional Cash Spent			
Sales Tax, VAT, HST/GST Paid Out	$0	$0	$0
Principal Repayment of Current Borrowing	$0	$0	$0
Other Liabilities Principal Repayment	$0	$0	$0
Long-term Liabilities Principal Repayment	$10,884	$10,884	$10,884
Purchase Other Current Assets	$0	$0	$0
Purchase Long-term Assets	$0	$0	$0
Dividends	$0	$0	$0
Subtotal Cash Spent	$321,785	$390,394	$424,564
Net Cash Flow	$328,215	$161,606	$102,985
Cash Balance	$349,215	$510,822	$613,807

Chart: Cash Flow

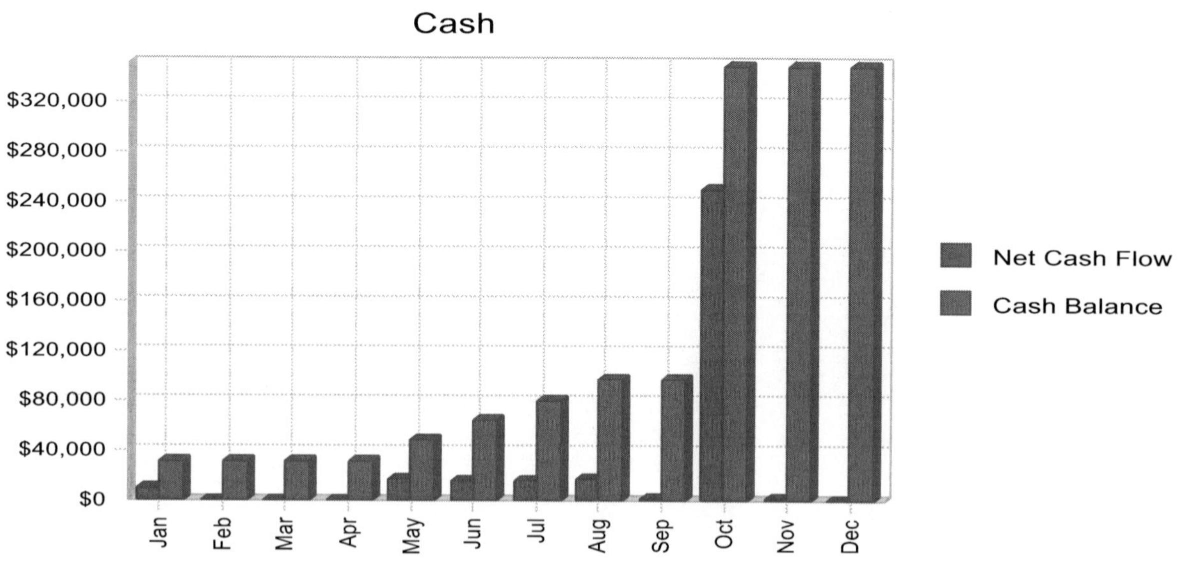

7.5 Projected Balance Sheet

The projected balance sheet for [Company Name]s LLC is shown on the table below.

Table: Balance Sheet

Pro Forma Balance Sheet		
	2010	2011
Assets		
Current Assets		
Cash	$349,215	$510,822
Other Current Assets	$247,000	$247,000
Total Current Assets	$596,215	$757,822
Long-term Assets		
Long-term Assets	$1,990,000	$1,990,000
Accumulated Depreciation	$0	$0
Total Long-term Assets	$1,990,000	$1,990,000
Total Assets	$2,586,215	$2,747,822
Liabilities and Capital	2010	2011
Current Liabilities		
Accounts Payable	$19,903	$21,702

Current Borrowing	$250,000	$350,000
Other Current Liabilities	$0	$0
Subtotal Current Liabilities	$269,903	$371,702
Long-term Liabilities	$653,116	$642,232
Total Liabilities	$923,019	$1,013,934
Paid-in Capital	$0	$0
Retained Earnings	$1,588,100	$1,663,196
Earnings	$75,096	$70,692
Total Capital	$1,663,196	$1,733,888
Total Liabilities and Capital	$2,586,215	$2,747,822
Net Worth	$1,663,196	$1,733,888

7.6 Business Ratios

Please find below the business ratios for the years of this plan. The Industry profile ratio is based on industry standard for "all other accommodations" with sales over $250,000 - $499,999

Table: Ratios

Ratio Analysis			
	2010	2011	Industry Profile
Sales Growth	16.97%	13.00%	4.33%
Percent of Total Assets			
Other Current Assets	9.55%	8.99%	22.99%
Total Current Assets	23.05%	27.58%	28.04%
Long-term Assets	76.95%	72.42%	71.96%
Total Assets	100.00%	100.00%	100.00%
Current Liabilities	10.44%	13.53%	12.54%
Long-term Liabilities	25.25%	23.37%	34.42%
Total Liabilities	35.69%	36.90%	46.96%
Net Worth	64.31%	63.10%	53.04%
Percent of Sales			
Sales	100.00%	100.00%	100.00%
Gross Margin	93.55%	94.18%	100.00%
Selling,	74.78%	78.54%	64.95%

General & Administrative Expenses			
Advertising Expenses	13.13%	11.62%	3.29%
Profit Before Interest and Taxes	40.10%	39.37%	1.03%
Main Ratios			
Current	2.21	2.04	1.13
Quick	2.21	2.04	0.86
Total Debt to Total Assets	35.69%	36.90%	58.34%
Pre-tax Return on Net Worth	5.31%	4.80%	1.59%
Pre-tax Return on Assets	3.42%	3.03%	0.66%
Additional Ratios	2010	2011	
Net Profit Margin	18.77%	15.64%	n.a
Return on Equity	4.52%	4.08%	n.a
Activity Ratios			
Accounts Payable Turnover	12.02	12.17	n.a
Payment Days	28	29	n.a

Total Asset Turnover	0.15	0.16	n.a
Debt Ratios			
Debt to Net Worth	0.55	0.58	n.a
Current Liab. to Liab.	0.29	0.37	n.a
Liquidity Ratios			
Net Working Capital	$326,312	$386,120	n.a
Interest Coverage	2.23	1.88	n.a
Additional Ratios			
Assets to Sales	6.47	6.08	n.a
Current Debt/Total Assets	10%	14%	n.a
Acid Test	2.21	2.04	n.a
Sales/Net Worth	0.24	0.26	n.a
Dividend Payout	0.00	0.00	n.a

B. How to Develop a Result Driven Business Plan

There are many reasons why a business plan should be prepared. Each is sufficient by itself for why one must go through the exercise of preparing the actual business plan. This guide discusses free small business plans, business plan outline. Regardless of the specific reason, the underlying goal of preparing a business plan is to insure the success of the business. Here are the main reasons why a business plan should be prepared:

Provides you with the road map that you need in order to run your business. It allows you to make detours, change directions, and alter the pace that you set in starting or running the business.

To assist in financing. Whether one is starting up a small business or is an entrepreneur, banks and financial institutions want to see that you know where you are, where you are going, and how you are going to get there.

The plan will tell you how much money you need, when you will need it, and how you are going to get it. In other words, how you will do your financing?

Helps you to clearly think through what type of business you are starting, and allows you to consider every aspect of that business.

Raises the questions that you need to have answered in order to succeed in your business.

Establishes a system of checks and balances for your business so that you avoid mistakes.

Sets up bench marks to keep your business under control.

Helps you develop the competitive spirit to make you keenly prepared and ready to operate.

Makes you think through the entire business process so that you do not open the business blindly or lack vital information in opening and maintaining your business.

Forces you to analyze competition.

Will give you a "go" or "no go" answer about starting the business.

Small Business Plans Business Plan Outline Guide

Below is an outline for a business plan. Use this model as a guide when developing the business plan for your business.

Elements of a Business Plan Outline:

1. Cover sheet

2. Executive Summary

3. Table of contents

A. The Business

(1) Description of business

(2) Marketing

(3) Competition

(4) Operating procedures

(5) Personnel

(6) Financial data

B. Financial Data

(1) Loan applications

(2) Capital equipment and supply list

(3) Balance sheet

(4) Break-even analysis

(5) Pro-Forma income projections (profit & loss statements)

* Three-year summary

* Detail by month first year

* Detail by quarters, second and third years

* Assumptions upon which projections were based

(6) Pro-forma cash flow

* Follow guidelines for (5).

C. Supporting Documents

Personal financial statement (all banks have these forms)

Copy of proposed lease or purchase agreement for building space

Copy of licenses and other legal documents

Copy of resumes of all principals

Copies of letters of intent from suppliers, etc.

Writing The Business Plan - What It Includes

What goes in a business plan? This is an excellent question to ask. And, one that many new and potential small business owners should ask, but oftentimes don't ask. The body of the business plan can be divided into four distinct sections:

1) The description of the business,

2) The marketing plan,

3) The financial management plan and

4) The management plan.

Addenda to the business plan should include the executive summary, supporting documents and financial projections.

Description of the business

In this section, provide a detailed description of your business. An excellent question to ask yourself is: "What business am I in?" In answering this question include your products, market and services as well as a thorough description of what makes your business unique. Remember, however, that as you develop your business plan, you may have to modify or revise your initial questions.

The business description section is divided into three primary sections.

Section 1 actually describes your business, Section 2 the product or service you will be offering and Section 3 the location of your business, and why this location is desirable.

1. Business Description

When describing your business, generally you should explain:

Legalities - business form: proprietorship, partnership, corporation, franchise. What licenses or permits you will need.

Business type: merchandising, manufacturing or service.

What your product or service is.

Is it a new independent business, a takeover, an expansion, a franchise?

Why your business will be profitable. What are the growth opportunities?

When your business will be open (days, hours).

What you have learned about your kind of business or franchise from outside sources (trade suppliers, bankers, other franchise owners, franchisor, publications).

A cover sheet goes before the description. It includes the name, address and telephone number of the business and the names of all principals. In the description of your business, describe the unique aspects and how or why they will appeal to consumers. Emphasize any special features that you feel will appeal to customers and explain how and why these features are appealing.

The description of your business should clearly identify goals and objectives and it should clarify why you are, or why you want to be, in business.

2. Product/Service

Try to describe the benefits of your goods and services from your customers' perspective.

Successful business owners know or at least have an idea of what their customers want or expect from them. This type of anticipation can be helpful in building customer satisfaction and loyalty. And, it certainly is a good strategy for beating the competition or retaining your competitiveness. Describe:

What you are selling.

How your product or service will benefit the customer.

Which products/services (in your case the franchise) are in demand; if there will be a steady flow of cash.

What is different about the product or service your franchise is offering.

3. The Location

The location of your business can play a decisive role in its success or failure. Your location should be built around your customers, it should be accessible and it should provide a sense of security. Consider these questions when addressing this section of your business plan:

What are your location needs?

What kind of space will you need?

Why is the area desirable? the building desirable?

Is it easily accessible? Is public transportation available? Is street lighting adequate?

Are market shifts or demographic shifts occurring?

It may be a good idea to make a checklist of questions you identify when developing your business plan. Categorize your questions and, as you answer each question, remove it from your list.

The Marketing Plan

Marketing plays a vital role in successful business ventures. How well you market your business, along with a few other considerations, will ultimately determine your degree of success or failure.

The key element of a successful marketing plan is to know your customers -- their likes, dislikes, expectations. By identifying these factors, you can develop a marketing strategy that will allow you to arouse and fulfill their needs.

Identify your customers by their age, sex, income/educational level and residence. At first, target only those customers who are more likely to purchase your product or service. As your customer base expands, you may need to consider modifying the marketing plan to include other customers.

Develop a marketing plan by answering these questions. Potential franchise owners will have to use the marketing strategy the franchisor has developed; however, it should be included in your business plan and contain answers to the questions outlined below.

Who are your customers? Define your target market(s).

Are your markets growing? steady? declining?

Is your franchise market share growing? steady? declining?

Has your franchisor segmented your markets?

Are your markets large enough to expand, depending on franchisor restrictions?

How will you attract, hold, increase your market share? Will the franchisor provide assistance in this area? Based on the franchisor's strategy, how will you promote your sales?

What pricing strategy, if any, has the franchisor devised?

1. Competition

Competition is a way of life. We compete for jobs, promotions, scholarships to institutes of higher learning, in sports -- and in almost every aspect of your lives. Nations compete for the consumer in the global marketplace as do individual business owners. Advances in technology can send the profit margins of a successful business into a tailspin causing them to plummet overnight or within a few hours.

When considering these and other factors, we can conclude that business is a highly competitive, volatile arena. Because of this volatility and competitiveness, it is important to know your competitors.

Questions like these can help you:

Who are your five nearest direct competitors?

Who are your indirect competitors?

How are their businesses: steady? increasing? decreasing?

What have you learned from their operations? from their advertising?

What are their strengths and weaknesses?

How does their product or service differ from yours?

Start a file on each of your competitors. Keep manila envelopes of their advertising and promotional materials and their pricing strategy techniques. Review these files periodically, determining when and how often they advertise, sponsor promotions and offer sales. Study the copy used in the advertising and promotional materials, and their sales strategy. For example, is their copy short? descriptive? catchy? or how much do they reduce prices for sales? Using this technique can help you to understand your competitors better and how they operate their businesses.

2. Pricing and Sales

Your pricing strategy is another marketing technique you can use to improve your overall competitiveness. It may be a good idea to get a feel for the pricing strategy your competitors are using. That way you can determine if your prices are in line with competitors in your market area and if they are in line with industry averages.

Some of the pricing strategies you may use, depending on the type of business, are:

Retail cost and pricing

Competitive position

Pricing below competition

Pricing above competition

Price lining

Multiple pricing

Service costs and pricing (for service businesses only)

Service components

Material costs

Labor costs

Overhead costs

The key to success is to have a well-planned strategy, to establish your policies and to constantly monitor prices and operating costs to ensure profits. It is a good policy to keep abreast of the changes in the marketplace because these changes can affect your competitiveness and profit margins.

3. Advertising and Public Relations

How you advertise and promote your business may make or break your business. Having a good product or service and not advertising and promoting it is like not having a business at all. Many business owners operate under the mistaken concept that the business will promote itself, and channel money that should be used for advertising and promotions to other areas of the business. Advertising and promotions, however, are the life line of a business and should be treated as such.

Devise a plan that uses advertising and networking as a means to promote your business. Develop short, descriptive copy (text material) that clearly identifies your goods or services, its location and price. Use catchy phrases to arouse the interest of your readers, listeners or viewers.

Make sure the advertisements you create are consistent with the image you are trying to project.

Remember the more care and attention you devote to your marketing program, the more successful your business will be.

Business Plan Outline Guide - The Management Plan

Managing a business requires more than just the desire to be your own boss. It demands dedication, persistence, the ability to make decisions and the ability to manage both employees and finances. Your management plan, along with your marketing and financial management plans, sets the foundation for and facilitates the success of your business.

Like plants and equipment, people are resources -- they are the most valuable asset a business has. You will soon discover that employees and staff will play an important role in the total operation of your business. Consequently, it's imperative that you know what skills you possess and those you lack since you will have to hire personnel to supply the skills that you lack. Additionally, it is imperative that you know how to manage and treat your employees. Make them a part of the team. Keep them informed of, and get their feedback regarding, changes. Employees oftentimes have excellent ideas that can lead to new market areas, innovations to existing products or services or new product lines or services which can improve your overall competitiveness.

Your management plan should answer questions such as:

How does your background/business experience help you in this business?

What are your weaknesses and how can you compensate for them?

Who will be on the management team?

What are their strengths/weaknesses?

What are their duties?

Are these duties clearly defined?

What are your current personnel needs?

What are your plans for hiring and training personnel?

What salaries, benefits, vacations, holidays will you offer?

What benefits, if any, can you afford at this point?

The Financial Management Plan

Sound financial management is one of the best ways for your business to remain profitable and solvent. How well you manage the finances of your business is the cornerstone of every successful business venture. Each year thousands of potentially successful businesses fail because of poor financial management. As a business owner, you will need to identify and implement policies that will lead to and ensure that you will meet your financial obligations.

To effectively manage your finances, plan a sound, realistic budget by determining the actual amount of money needed to open your business (start-up costs) and the amount needed to keep it open (operating costs). The first step to building a sound financial plan is to devise a start-up budget. Your start-up budget will usually include such one-time-only costs as major equipment, utility deposits, down payments, etc.

The start-up budget should allow for these expenses.

Start-up Budget

Personnel (costs prior to opening)

Legal/professional fees

Occupancy

Equipment

Supplies

Salaries/wages

Income

Utilities

Payroll expenses

Licenses/permits

Insurance

Advertising/promotions

Accounting

An operating budget is prepared when you are actually ready to open for business. The operating budget will reflect your priorities in terms of how your spend your money, the expenses you will incur and how you will meet those expenses (income). Your operating budget also should include money to cover the first three to six months of operation. It should allow for the following expenses.

Operating Budget

Personnel

Rent

Loan payments

Legal/accounting

Supplies

Salaries/wages

Dues/subscriptions/fees

Repairs/maintenance

Insurance

Advertising/promotions

Depreciation

Payroll expenses

Taxes

Miscellaneous expenses

The financial section of your business plan should include any loan applications you've filed, a capital equipment and supply list, balance sheet, break-even analysis, pro-forma income projections (profit and loss statement) and pro-forma cash flow.

The income statement and cash flow projections should include a three-year summary, detail by month for the first year, and detail by quarter for the second and third years.

The accounting system and the inventory control system that you will be using is generally addressed in this section of the business plan also. Whether you develop the accounting and inventory systems yourself, have an outside financial advisor develop the systems, you will need to acquire a thorough understanding of each and how it operates. Your financial advisor can assist you in developing this section of your business plan.

The following questions should help you determine the amount of start-up capital you will need to purchase and open your business.

How much money do you have?

How much money will you need for start-up?

How much money will you need to stay in business?Other questions that you will need to consider are:

What type of accounting system will your use? Is it a single entry or dual entry system?

What will your sales goals and profit goals for the coming year be?

What financial projections will you need to include in your business plan?

What kind of inventory control system will you use?

Your plan should include an explanation of all projections. Unless you are thoroughly familiar with financial statements, get help in preparing your cash flow and income statements and your balance sheet. Your aim is not to become a financial wizard, but to understand the financial tools well enough to gain their benefits. Your accountant or financial advisor can help you accomplish this goal.

C. How to Attract Investors

Venture capital financing is a method used for Raising Cash For Business and Getting Investments for Business, but less popular than borrowing. Venture capital firms, like banks, supply you with the funds necessary to operate your business, but they do it differently. Banks are creditors; they expect you to repay the borrowed money. Venture capital firms are owners; they hold stock in the company, adding their invested capital to its equity base. While banks may concentrate on cash flow, venture capital firms invest for long-term capital. Commonly, these firms look for their investment to appreciate three to five times in five or seven years.

One way of explaining the different ways in which banks and venture capital firms evaluate a small business seeking funds is: Banks look at its immediate future, but are most heavily influenced by its past; venture capitalists look to its longer run future.

To be sure, venture capital firms and individuals are interested in many of the same factors that influence bankers in their analysis of loan applications from smaller companies. All financial people want to know the results and ratios of past operations, the amount and intended use of the needed funds, and the earnings and financial condition of future projections.

But venture capitalists look much more closely at the features of the product and the size of the market than do commercial banks.

What Venture Capital Firms Look For

Banks are creditors. They're interested in the product/market position of the company for assurance that this product or service can provide steady sales and generate sufficient cash flow to repay the loan. They look at projections to be certain that owners/managers have done their homework.

Venture capital firms are owners. They hold stock in the company, adding their invested capital to its equity base. Therefore, they examine existing or planned products or services and the potential markets for them with extreme care. They invest only in firms they believe can rapidly increase sales and generate substantial profits. The reason for this is that venture capital firms invest for long-term capital, not for interest income. A common estimate is that they look for three to five times their investment in five or seven years.

Of course, venture capitalists don't realize capital gains on all their investments. Certainly they don't make capital gains of 300 to 500% except on a very limited portion of their total investments. But their intent is to find venture projects with this appreciation potential to make up for investments that aren't successful.

Venture capital is risky due to the difficulty of judging the worth of a business in its early stages. Therefore, most venture capital firms set rigorous policies for venture proposal size, maturity of the seeking company, management of the seeking company, and "something special" in the plan that is submitted. They also have rigorous evaluation procedures to reduce risks, since their investments are unprotected in the event of failure.

Size of the Venture Proposal

Most venture capital firms are interested in investment projects requiring an investment of $250,000 to $1,500,000. Projects requiring under $250,000 are of limited interest because of the high cost of investigation and administration; however, some venture capital firms will consider smaller proposals if the investment is intriguing enough.

The typical venture capital firm receives over 400 proposals a year. Probably 90% of these will be rejected quickly because they don't fit the established geographical, technical or market area policies of the firm - or because they have been poorly prepared.

The remaining 10% are carefully investigated. These investigations are expensive. Firms may hire consultants to evaluate the product, particularly when it is the result of innovation or is technologically complex. The market size and competitive position of the company are analyzed by contacts with present and potential customers, suppliers, and others. Production costs are reviewed. The financial condition of the company is confirmed by an auditor. The legal form and registration of the business are checked. Most importantly, the character and competence of the management are evaluated by the venture capital firm, normally via a thorough background check.

These preliminary investigations may cost a venture firm between $2,000 and $3,000 per company investigated. They result in perhaps ten to fifteen proposals of interest. Then, second investigations, more thorough and more expensive than the first, reduce the number of proposals under consideration to only three or four. Eventually, the firm invests in one or two of these.

Most venture capital firms' investment interest is limited to projects proposed by companies with some operating history, even though they may not yet have shown a profit. Companies that can expand into a new product line or a new market with additional funds are particularly interesting. The venture capital firm can provide funds to enable such companies to grow in a spurt rather than gradually as they would on retained earnings. Raising Money From Investors.

Companies that are just starting or that have serious financial difficulties may interest some venture capitalists, if the potential for significant gain over the long run can be identified and assessed. If the venture firm has already extended its portfolio to a large risk concentration, they may be reluctant to invest in these areas because of increased risk of loss.

Although most venture capital firms will not consider a great many proposals from start-up companies, there are a small number of venture firms that will do "start-up" financing. The small firm that has a well thought-out plan and can demonstrate that its management group has an outstanding record (even if it is with other companies) has a decided edge in acquiring this kind of seed capital.

Most venture capital firms concentrate primarily on the competence and character of the management. They feel that even mediocre products can be successfully manufactured, promoted, and distributed by an experienced, energetic management group.

They look for a group that is able to work together easily and productively, especially under conditions of stress from temporary reversals and competition problems. Obviously, analysis of managerial skill is difficult. A partner or senior executive of a venture capital firm normally spends at least a week at the offices of a company being considered, talking with and observing the management to estimate their competence and character.

Venture capital firms usually require that the company under consideration have a complete management group. Each of the important functional areas product design, marketing, production, finance, and control - must be under the direction of a trained, experienced member of the group. Responsibilities must be clearly assigned. And, in addition to a thorough understanding of the industry, each member of the management team must be firmly committed to the company and its future.

Next in importance to the excellence of the management group, most venture capital firms seek a distinctive element in the strategy or product/market/process position of the company. This distinctive element may be a new feature of the product or process or a particular skill or technical competence of the management. But it must exist. It must provide a competitive advantage.

Elements of a Venture Proposal

Purpose and Objectives

Include a summary of the what and why of the project.

Proposed Financing: You must state the amount of money you will need from the beginning to the maturity of the project proposed, how the proceeds will be used, how you plan to structure the financing, and why the amount designated is required.

Marketing: Describe the market segment you've got or plan to get, the competition, the characteristics of the market, and your plans (with costs) for getting or holding the market segment you're aiming at.

History of the Firm: Summarize the significant financial and organizational milestones,

Description of employees and employee relations, explanations of banking relationships, recounting of major services or products your firm has offered during its existence, and the like.

Description of the Product or Service: Include a full description of the product (process) or service offered by the firm and the costs associated with it in detail.

Financial Statements: Include statements for both the past few years and pro forma projections (balance sheets, income statements, and cash flows) for the next three to five years, showing the effect anticipated if the project is undertaken and if the financing is secured. (This should include an analysis of key variables affecting financial performance, showing what could happen if the projected level of revenue is not attained.)

Capitalization: Provide a list of shareholders, how much is invested to date, and in what form (equity/debt).

Biographical Sketches: Describe the work histories and qualifications of key owners and employees.

Principal Suppliers and Customers, Problems Anticipated and Other Pertinent Information

Provide a candid discussion of any contingent liabilities, pending litigation, tax or patent difficulties, and any other contingencies that might affect the project you're proposing. List the names, addresses and the

Telephone numbers of suppliers and customers; they will be contacted to verify your statement about payments (suppliers) and products (customers).

Provisions of the Investment Proposal

What happens when, after the exhaustive investigation and analysis, the venture capital firms decides to invest in a company? Most venture firms prepare an equity financing proposal that details the amount of money to be provided, the percentage of common stock to be surrendered in exchange for these funds, the interim financing method to be used and the protective covenants to be included.

This proposal will be discussed with the management of the company. The final financing agreement will be negotiated and generally represents a compromise between the management of the company and the partners or senior executives of the venture capital firm. The important elements of this compromise are: ownership, control, annual charges, and final objectives.

Ownership

Venture capital financing is not inexpensive for the owners of a small business. The partners of the venture firm buy a portion of the business' equity in exchange for their investment.

This percentage of equity varies, of course, and depends on the amount of money provided, the success and worth of the business, and the anticipated investment return. It can range from perhaps 10% in the case of an established, profitable company to as much as 80 or 90% for beginning or financially troubled firms.

Most venture capital firms, at least initially, don't want a position of more than 30 to 40% because they want the owner to have the incentive to keep building the business. If additional financing is required to support

Business growth, the outsiders' stake may exceed 50% but investors realize that small business owner/managers can lose their entrepreneurial zeal under those circumstances. In the final analysis, however, the venture firm, regardless of its percentage of ownership, really wants to leave control in the hands of the company's managers because it is really investing in that management team in the first place.

Most venture firms determine the ratio of funds provided to equity requested by a comparison of the present financial worth of the contributions made by each of the parties to the agreement. The present value of the contribution by the owner of a starting or financially troubled company is obviously rated low. Often it is estimated as just the existing value of his or her idea and the competitive costs of the owner's time. The contribution by the owners of a thriving business is valued much higher. Generally, it is capitalized at a multiple of the current earnings and/or net worth.

Financial valuation is not an exact science. The final compromise on the worth of the owner's contribution in the equity financing agreement is likely to be much lower than the owner thinks it should be and considerably higher than the partners of the capital firm think it might be. In the ideal situation, of course, the two parties to the agreement are able to do together what neither could do separately: 1) the company is able to grow fast enough with the additional funds to do more than overcome the owner's loss of equity; and 2) the investment grows at a sufficient rate to compensate the venture capitalists for assuming the risk.

An equity financing agreement with an outcome in five to seven years which pleases both parties is ideal. Since the parties cannot see this outcome in the present, neither will be perfectly satisfied with the compromise reached.

It is important, though, for the business owner to look at the future. He or she should carefully consider the impact of the ratio of funds invested to the ownership given up, not only for the present, but for the years to come.

Control

Control is a much simpler issue to resolve. Unlike the division of ownership over which the venture firm and management are likely to disagree, control is an issue in which they have a common interest. While it is understandable that the management of a small company will have some anxiety in this area, the partners of a venture firm have little interest in assuming control of the business. They have neither the technical nor the managerial personnel to run a number of small companies in diverse industries. They much prefer to leave operating control to the existing management.

The venture capital firm does, however, want to participate in any strategic decisions that might change the basic product/market character of the company and in any major investment decisions that might divert or deplete the financial resources of the company. They will, therefore, generally ask that at least one partner be made a director of the company.

They also want to be able to assume control and attempt to rescue their investment if severe financial, operating or marketing problems

Develop. Thus, they will usually include protective covenants in their equity financing agreements to permit them to take control and appoint new officers if financial performance is very poor.

Annual Charges

The investment of the venture capital firm may be in the final form of direct stock ownership which does not impose fixed charges. More likely, it will be in an interim form - convertible subordinated debentures or preferred stock. Financings may also be straight loans with options or warrants that can be converted to a future equity position at a pre-established price.

The convertible debenture form of financing is like a loan. The debentures can be converted at an established ratio to the common stock of the company within a given period, so that the venture capital firm can prepare to realize their capital gains at their option in the future. These instruments are often subordinated to existing and planned debt to permit the company invested in to obtain additional bank financing.

Debentures also provide additional security and control for the venture firm and impose a fixed charge for interest (and possibly principal) on the company. The owner/manager of a small company seeking equity financing should consider the burden of any fixed annual charges resulting from the financing agreement.

Final Objectives

Venture capital firms generally intend to realize capital gains on their investments by providing for a stock buy-back by the small firm, by arranging a public offering of stock of the company invested in or by providing for a merger with a larger firm that has publicly traded stock. They usually hope to do this within five to seven years of their initial investment. (It should be noted that several additional stages of financing may be required over this period of time.)

Most equity financing agreements include provisions guaranteeing that the venture capital firm may participate in any stock sale or approve any merger, regardless of their percentage of stock ownership. Sometimes the agreement will require that the management work toward an eventual stock sale or merger. Clearly, the owner/manager of a small company seeking equity financing must consider the future impact upon his or her own stock holdings and personal ambition of the venture firm's aims, since taking in a venture capitalist as a partner may be virtually a commitment to eventually sell out or go public.

Types of Venture Capital Firms

Traditional Partnerships are often established by wealthy families to aggressively manage a portion of their funds by investing in small companies.

Professionally Managed Pools are made up of institutional money and which operate like the traditional partnerships.

Investment Banking Firms usually trade in more established securities, but occasionally form investor syndicates for venture proposals.

Insurance Companies often have required a portion of equity as a condition of their loans to smaller companies as protection against inflation.

Manufacturing Companies have sometimes looked upon investing in smaller companies as a means of supplementing their research and development programs.

In addition to these venture capital firms, there are individual private investors and finders. Finders, which can be firms or individuals, often know the capital industry and may be able to help the small company seeking capital to locate it, though they are generally not sources of capital themselves. Care should be exercised so that a small business owner deals with reputable, professional finders whose fees are in line with industry practice. Further, it should be noted that venture capitalists generally prefer working directly with principals in making investments, though finders may provide useful introductions.

The Importance of Formal Financial Planning

In case there is any doubt about the implications of the previous sections, it should be noted that it is extremely difficult for any small firm especially the starting or struggling company - to get venture capital.

There is one thing, however, that owner/managers of small businesses can do to improve the chances of their venture proposals at least escaping the 90% which are almost immediately rejected. In a word - plan.

Having financial plans demonstrates to venture capital firms that you are a competent manager, that you may have that special managerial edge over other small business owners looking for equity money. You may gain a decided advantage through well-prepared plans and projections that include: cash budgets, pro forma statements, and capital investment analysis and capital source studies.

Cash budgets should be projected for one year and prepared monthly.

They should combine expected sales revenues, cash receipts, material, labor and overhead expenses, and cash disbursements on a monthly basis. This permits anticipation of fluctuations in the level of cash and planning for short term borrowing and investment.

Pro forma statements should be prepared for planning up to three years ahead. They should include both income statements and balance sheets.

Again, these should be prepared quarterly to combine expected sales revenues; production, marketing and administrative expenses; profits; product, market or process investments; and supplier, bank or investment company borrowings. Pro forma statements permit you to anticipate the financial results of your operations and to plan intermediate term borrowings and investments.

Capital investment analyses and capital source studies should be prepared for planning up to five years ahead. The investment analyses should compare rate of return for product, market, or process investment, while the source alternatives should compare the cost and availability of debt and equity and the expected level of retained earnings, which together will support the selected investments. These analyses and source studies should be prepared quarterly so you may anticipate the financial consequences of changes in your company's strategy. They will allow you to plan long term borrowings, equity placements, and major investments.

There is a bonus in making such projections. They force you to consider the results of your actions. Your estimates must be explicit; you have to examine and evaluate your managerial records; disagreements must be resolved - or at least discussed and understood. Financial planning may be burdensome but it is one of the keys to business success.

Now, making these financial plans will not guarantee that you'll be able to get venture capital. Not making them will virtually assure that you won't receive favorable consideration from venture capitalists.

D. How to Obtain Business Loans the Easy Way

Some businesspersons cannot understand why a lending institution refused to lend them money. Others have no trouble getting funds, but are surprised to find strings attached to their loans. Such owner-managers fail to realize that banks and other lenders have to operate by certain principles just as do other types of business.

This Guide discusses the following fundamentals of borrowing: (1) credit worthiness, (2) kinds of loans, (3) amount of money needed, (4) collateral, (5) loan restrictions and limitation, (6) the loan application, and (7) standards which the lender uses to evaluate the application.

Introduction

Inexperience with borrowing procedures often created resentment and bitterness. The stories of three businesspersons illustrate this point.

"I'll never trade here again," Bill Smith said when his bank refused to grant him a loan. "I'd like to let you have it, Bill," the banker said, "but your firm isn't earning enough to meet your current obligations." Mr. Smith was unaware of a vital financial fact, namely, that lending institutions have to be certain that the borrower's business can repay the loan.

Tom Jones lost his temper when the bank refused him a loan because he did not know what kind of or how much money he needed. "We hesitate to lend," the banker said, "to business owners with such vague ideas of what and how much they need."

John William's' case was somewhat different. He didn't explode until after he got the loan. When the papers were ready to sign, he realized that the loan agreement put certain limitations on his business activities. "You can't dictate to me," he said and walked out of the bank. What he didn't realize was that the limitations were for his good as well as for the bank's protection.

Knowledge of the financial facts of business life could have saved all three the embarrassment of losing their tempers. Even more important, such information would have helped them to borrow money at a time when their businesses needed it badly.

This Guide is designed to give the highlights of what is involved in sound business borrowing. It should be helpful to those who have little or no experience with borrowing. More experienced owner-managers should find it useful in re-evaluating their borrowing operations.

Is Your Firm Credit Worthy?

The ability to obtain money when you need it is as necessary to the operation of your business as is a good location or the right equipment, reliable sources of supplies and materials, or an adequate labor force. Before a bank or any other lending agency will lend you money, the loan officer must feel satisfied with the answers to the five following questions:

1. What sort of person are you, the prospective borrower? By all odds, the character of the borrower comes first. Next is your ability to manage your business.

2. What are you going to do with the money? The answer to this question will determine the type of loan, short or long-term. Money to be used for the purchase of seasonal inventory will require quicker repayment than money used to buy fixed assets.

3. When and how do you plan to pay it back? Your banker's judgment of your business ability and the type of loan will be a deciding factor in the answer to this question.

4. Is the cushion in the loan large enough? In other words, does the amount requested make suitable allowance for unexpected developments? The banker decides this question on the basis of your financial statement which sets forth the condition of your business and on the collateral pledged.

5. What is the outlook for business in general and for your business particularly?

Adequate Financial Data Is a "Must"

The banker wants to make loans to businesses which are solvent, profitable, and growing. The two basic financial statements used to determine those conditions are the balance sheet and profit-and-loss statement. The former is the major yardstick for solvency and the latter for profits. A continuous series of these two statements over a period of time is the principal device for measuring financial stability and growth potential.

In interviewing loan applicants and in studying their records the banker is especially interested in the following facts and figures.

General Information: Are the books and records up-to-date and in good condition? What is the condition of accounts payable? Of notes payable? What are the salaries of the owner-manager and other company officers? Are all taxes being paid currently? what is the order backlog? What is the insurance coverage?

Accounts Receivable: Are there indications that some of the accounts receivable have already been pledged to another creditor? What is the accounts receivable turnover? Is the accounts receivable total weakened because many customers are far behind in their payments? Has a large enough reserve been set up to cover doubtfull accounts? How much do the largest accounts owe and what percentage of your total accounts does this amount represent?

Inventories: Is merchandise in good shape or will it have to be marked down? How much raw material is on hand? How much work is in process? How much of the inventory is finished goods?

Is there any obsolete inventory? Has an excessive amount of inventory been consigned to customers? Is inventory turnover in line with the turnover for other businesses in the same industry? Or is money being tied up too long in inventory?

Fixed Assets: What is the type, age, and condition of the equipment? What are the depreciation policies? What are the details of mortgages or conditional sales contracts? What are the future acquisition plans?

What Kind Of Money?

When you set out to borrow money for your firm, it is important to know the kind of money you need from a bank or other lending institution. There are three kinds of money: short term, term money, and equity capital.

Keep in mind that the purpose for which the funds are to be used is an important factor in deciding the kind of money needed. But even so, deciding what kind of money to use is not always easy. It is sometimes complicated by the fact that you may be using some of the various kinds of money at the same time and for identical purposes.

Keep in mind that a very important distinction between the types of money is the source of repayment. Generally short-term loans are repaid from the liquidation of current assets which they have financed. Long-term loans are usually repaid from earnings.

Short-Term Bank Loans

You can use short-term bank loans for purposes such as financing accounts receivable for, say 30 to 60 days. Or you can use them for purposes that take longer to pay off - such as for building a seasonal inventory over a period of 5 to 6 months. Usually, lenders expect short-term loans to be repaid after their purposes have been served: for example, accounts receivable loans, when the outstanding accounts have been paid by the borrower's customers, and inventory loans, when the inventory has been converted into salable merchandise.

Banks grant such money either on your general credit reputation with an unsecured loan or on a secured loan.

The unsecured loan is the most frequently used form of bank credit for short term purposes. You do not have to put up collateral because the bank relies on your credit reputation.

The secured loan involves a pledge of some or all of your assets. The bank requires security as a protection for its depositors against the risks that are involved even in business situations where the chances of success are good.

Term Borrowing

Term borrowing provides money you plan to pay back over a fairly long time. Some people break it down into two forms: (1) intermediate - loans longer than 1 year but less than 5 years, and (2) long-term - loan for more than 5 years.

However, for your purpose of matching the kind of money to the needs of your company, think of term borrowing as a kind of money which you probably will pay back in periodic installments from earnings.

Equity Capital

Some people confuse term borrowing and equity (or investment) capital. Yet there is a big difference. You don't have to repay equity money. It is money you get by selling a part interest in your business.

You take people into your company who are willing to risk their money in it. They are interested in potential income rather than in an immediate return on their investment.

How Much Money?

The amount of money you need to borrow depends on the purpose for which you need funds. Figuring the amount of money required for business construction, conversion, or expansion - term loans or equity capital - is relatively easy. Equipment manufacturers, architects, and builders will readily supply you with cost estimates.

On the other hand, the amount of working capital you need depends upon the type of business you're in. While rule-of-thumb ratios may be helpful as a starting point, a detailed projection of sources and uses of funds over some future period of time - usually for 12 months - is a better approach.

In this way, the characteristics of the particular situation can be taken into account. Such a projection is developed through the combination of a predicted budget and a cash forecast.

The budget is based on recent operating experience plus your best judgment of performance during the coming period. The cash forecast is your estimates of cash receipts and disbursements during the budget period. Thus, the budget and the cash forecast together represent your plan for meeting your working capital requirements.

To plan your working capital requirements, it is important to know the "cash flow" which your business will generate. This involves simply a consideration of all elements of cash receipts and disbursements at the time they occur. These elements are listed in the profit-and-loss statement which has been adapted to show cash flow. They should be projected for each month.

What Kind of Collateral?

Sometimes, your signature is the only security the bank needs when making a loan. At other times, the bank requires additional assurance that the money will be repaid. The kind and amount of security depends on the bank and on the borrower's situation.

If the loan required cannot be justified by the borrower's financial statements alone, a pledge of security may bridge the gap. The types of security are: endorsers; co-makers and guarantors; assignment of leases; trust receipts and floor planning; chattel mortgages; real estate; accounts receivables; saving accounts; life insurance policies; and stocks and bonds. In a substantial number of States where the Uniform Commercial Code has been enacted, paperwork for recording loan transactions will be greatly simplified.

Endorsers, Co-makers, and Guarantors

Borrowers often get other people to sign a note in order to bolster their own credit.

These endorsers are contingently liable for the note they sign. If the borrower fails to pay up, the bank expects the endorser to make the note good. Sometimes, the endorser may be asked to pledge assets or securities too.

A co-maker is one who creates an obligation jointly with the borrower. In such cases, bank can collect directly from either the maker or the co-maker.

A guarantor is one who guarantees the payment of a note by signing a guaranty commitment. Both private and government lenders often require guarantees from offices of corporations in order to assure continuity of effective management. Sometimes, a manufacturer will act as guarantor for customers.

Assignment of Leases

The assigned lease as security is similar to the guarantee. It is used, for example, in some franchise situations.

The bank lends the money on a building and takes a mortgage. Then the lease, which the dealer and the parent franchise company work out, is assigned so that the bank automatically receives the rent payments. In this manner, the bank is guaranteed repayment of the loan.

Warehouse Receipts

Banks also take commodities as security by lending money on a warehouse receipt. Such a receipt is usually delivered directly to the bank and shows that the merchandise used as security either has been placed in a public warehouse or has been left on your premises under the control of one of your employees who is bonded (as in field warehousing). Such loans are generally made on staple or standard merchandise which can be readily marketed. The typical warehouse receipt loan is for a percentage of the estimated value of the goods used as security.

Trust Receipts and Floor Planning

Merchandise, such as automobiles, appliances, and boats, has to be displayed to be sold. The only way many small marketers can afford such displays is by borrowing money. Such loans are often secured by a note and a trust receipt.

This trust receipt is the legal paper for floor planning. It is used for serial-numbered merchandise. When you sign one, you (1) acknowledge receipt of the merchandise, (2) agree to keep the merchandise in trust for the bank, and (3) promise to pay the bank as you sell the goods.

Chattel Mortgages

If you buy equipment such as a cash register or a delivery truck, you may want to get a chattel mortgage loan. You give the bank a lien on the equipment you are buying.

The bank also evaluates the present and future market value of the equipment being used to secure the loan. How rapidly will it depreciate? Does the borrower have the necessary fire, theft, property damage, and public liability insurance on the equipment? The banker has to be sure that the borrower protects the equipment.

Real Estate

Real estate is another form of collateral for long-term loans. When taking a real estate mortgage, the bank finds out: (1) the location of the real estate, (2) its physical condition, (3) its foreclosure value, and (4) the amount of insurance carried on the property.

Accounts Receivable

Many banks lend money on accounts receivable. In effect, you are counting on your customers to pay your note.

The bank may take accounts receivable on a notification or a non-notification plan.

Under the notification plan, the purchaser of the goods is informed by the bank that his or her account has been assigned to it and he or she is asked to pay the bank. Under the non-notification plan, the borrower's customers continue to pay you the sums due on their accounts and you pay the bank.

Savings Accounts

Sometimes, you might get a loan by assigning to the bank a savings account. In such cases, the bank gets an assignment from you and keeps your passbook. If you assign an account in another bank as collateral, the lending bank asks the other bank to mark its records to show that the account is held as collateral.

Life Insurance

Another kind of collateral is life insurance. Banks will lend up to the cash value of a life insurance policy. You have to assign the policy to the bank.

If the policy is on the life of an executive of a small corporation, corporate resolutions must be made authorizing the assignment. Most insurance companies allow you to sign the policy back to the original beneficiary when the assignment to the bank ends.

Some people like to use life insurance as collateral rather than borrow directly from insurance companies. One reason is that a bank loan is often more convenient to obtain and usually may be obtained at a lower interest rate.

Stocks and Bonds

If you use stocks and bonds as collateral, they must be marketable. As a protection against market declines and possible expenses of liquidation, banks usually lend no more than 75 percent of the market value of high grade stock. On Federal Government or municipal bonds, they may be willing to lend 90 percent or more of their market value.

The bank may ask the borrower for additional security or payment whenever the market value of the stocks or bonds drops below the bank's required margin.

What Are the Lender's Rules?

Lending institutions are not interested in loan repayments. They are interested in borrowers with healthy profit-making businesses.

Therefore, whether or not collateral is required for a loan, they set loan limitation and restrictions to protect themselves against unnecessary risks and at the same time against poor management practices by their borrowers. Often some owner-managers consider loan limitations a burden.

Yet others feel that such limitation also offer an opportunity for improving their management techniques.

Especially in making long-term loans, the borrower as well as the lender should be thinking of: (1) the net earning power of the borrowing company, (2) the capability of its management, (3) the long range prospects of the company, and (4) the long range prospects of the industry of which the company is a part. Such factors often mean that limitation increase as the duration of the loan increases.

What Kinds of Limitation?

The kinds of limitations, which an owner-manager finds set upon the company depends, to a great extent, on the company. If the company is a good risk, only minimum limitations need be set. A poor risk, of course, is different. Its limitation should be greater than those of a stronger company.

Look now for a few moments at the kinds of limitations and restrictions which the lender may set. Knowing what they are can help you see how they affect your operations.

The limitations which you will usually run into when you borrow money are:

(1) Repayment terms.

(2) Pledging or the use of security.

(3) Periodic reporting.

A loan agreement, as you may already know, is a tailor-made document covering, or referring to, all the terms and conditions of the loan.

With it, the lender does two things: (1) protects position as a creditor (keeps that position in as protected a state as it was on the date the loan was made) and (2) assures repayment according to the terms.

The lender reasons that the borrower's business should generate enough funds to repay the loan while taking care of other needs. The lender considers that cash inflow should be great enough to do this without hurting the working capital of the borrower.

Covenants - Negative and Positive

The actual restrictions in a loan agreement come under a section known as covenants. Negative covenants are things which the borrower may not do without prior approval from the lender. Some examples are: further additions to the borrower's total debt, non-pledge to others of the borrower's assets and issuance of dividends in excess of the terms of the loan agreement

On the other hand, positive covenants spell out things which the borrower must do. Some examples are: (1) maintenance of a minimum net working capital, (2) carrying of adequate insurance, (3) repaying the loan according to the terms of the agreement, and (4) supplying the lender with financial statements and reports.

Overall, however, loan agreements may be amended from time to time and exceptions made. Certain provisions may be waived from one year to the next with the consent of the lender.

You Can Negotiate

Next time you go to borrow money, thrash out the lending terms before you sign. It is good practice no matter how badly you may need the money.

Ask to see the papers in advance of the loan closing. Legitimate lenders are glad to cooperate.

Chances are that the lender may "give" some on the terms. Keep in mind also that, while your are mulling over the terms, you may want to get the advice of your associates and outside advisors.

In short, try to get terms which you know your company can live with. Remember, however that once the terms have been agreed upon and the loan is made you are bound by them.

The Loan Application

Now that you have read about the various aspects of the lending process and are ready to apply for a loan. Banks and other private lending institutions, require a loan application on which you list certain information about your business

Evaluating the Application

Once you have supplied the necessary information, the next step in the borrowing process is the evaluation of your application. The officer considers this kind of thing when determining whether to grant or refuse the loan:

(1) The borrower's debt paying record to suppliers, banks, home mortgage holders, and other creditors.

(2) The ratio of the borrower's debt to net worth.

(3) The past earnings of the company.

(4) The value and conditions of the collateral which the borrower offers for security.

E. How to Effectively Manage Your Loans

Poor management is the reason why some owner-managers have trouble when they try to borrow. Those managers often fail to forecast and to plan for cash needs. The resulting business ailment is a "cash crisis."

Sound management must be practiced if loans are to be obtained and used profitably. Such management included: knowing the firm's cash flow, forecasting cash needs, planning to borrow at the appropriate time, and substantiating the firm's payback ability.

This Guide includes examples of the following: a cash budget forecast, a projection of borrowing requirements, and a cash flow schedule for repaying a loan.

In spite of respectable sales volumes, many owners of businesses run into financial trouble. Some get in so deep that they are barely able to pull their heads back above water. Others find themselves only weeks or months away from tacking "out of business" signs on their doors.

Often these owner-managers have three things in common. First, they know their line of business. Their technical ability is first rate. Second, they are poor managers. In many instances, they fail to plan ahead because of their enthusiasm for the operating side of their business. In the third place, most of them feel that additional money will solve their problems. They think that a loan will pull them out of the red.

Lending Officer's Viewpoint

Often a bank lending officer refuses or "declines" that loan request of such manager-owners. It is not that a banker lacks appreciation for the hard work and long hours which these owners put into their businesses. Nor does the bank question their good intentions.

Foremost in the lender's mind is the question: Can the firm pay back the loan? Thus, in many cases, the lender refuses the loan because the owner-manager hastily and haphazardly prepared the loan application under pressuring circumstances. As a result, the lending officer detects an air of instability and lack of planning in the owner-manager's description of his or her affairs. "How is the borrower really going to repay," the lending officer asks, "if the borrower doesn't actually know how much money is needed and how it is going to be used?"

If your request for a loan is turned down, the best bet is to accept the refusal gracefully and look for weaknesses in the presentation, You can correct these weaknesses when applying for a loan in the future.

Pertinent Questions

The lender needs the answers to several pertinent questions to determine whether or not the borrower can repay the loan. One of these questions is: What does the borrower intend to use the money for?

What Kind of Money? When you consider borrowing determine what kind of money you need. A business uses four basic types of money in its operations. Your purpose in borrowing will determine the type.

1. **Trade Credit.** This type of "money" is not borrowed. It is money you owe your suppliers who permit you to carry your fast-moving inventory on open account. A good credit experience is proven evidence of your ability to repay borrowed funds.

2. **Short-Term Credit.** Banks and other lenders will provide this type of money to carry you in your purchases of inventory for special reasons, such as buying inventory for the next selling season. Such loans are self-liquidating because they generate sales dollars. You repay short-term credit in less than a year.

3. Long-Term Credit. Such loans - for more than a year - are used for expansion or modernization of your business. They are repaid out of accumulated profits. Usually, the evidence of this type of loan in a business is a mortgage or a promissory note with terms.

4. Equity Funds. This type of money is never repaid. You get it by relinquishing a part of your profits to an investor. That is you sell an interest in your business.

Many owner-managers fail to recognize the difference between the four types of money. You should keep in mind that money borrowed for a temporary purpose should be used in the profit producing areas of your business and will be repaid out of that operation. Equity funds are those which remain in the business and increase the net worth for the owner.

Are Your Sales Adequate? Are you asking for a loan to bolster sagging sales volume? To buy additional stocks of high-volume merchandise which you feel has even greater potential? To create a new image by an over-all advertising campaign?

What Is Your Receivables Position? Are your accounts going uncollected and getting old? In effect, do you really need money to carry old accounts?

Is Your Profit Margin Adequate? Are you doing a lot of business and showing a lack of profit thus indicating that expenses are not controlled? Or is your market insufficient? What is your break-even point for profits?

What Is Your Plan For Repayment? Do you forecast your cash income and expenditures realistically?

The lender scrutinizes the cash flow of the business to determine whether or not the owner-manager is providing sufficient cash to meet the firm's obligations. The lender also has to make sure that cash needed for working capital is not being absorbed by the business into other areas of equity and thereby reducing liquidity.

The "Cash Crisis"

The experience of counselors is that all too often the business owner feels that his or her needs are financial when they are actually managerial. In such firms, money can ease the pressure temporarily, but further indebtedness only intensifies the basic problem. Money alone cannot provide the sound management needed to continue the business.

Counselors to business owners are continually faced with the "cash crisis" problem. This cash deficiency results from the lack of planning.

A mistake many purchasers of a business make is that they buy something beyond their means. They take possession of a business of some value but without one important asset - sufficient operating cash. When a buyer does not put aside working capital (cash), he or she cannot pay current bills and the rest of the story is easy to foretell.

It is the "cash crisis."

Sound management consists of arranging matters so that current liabilities are provided for as they become due and hence paid promptly. When such coordination is not present, the result is a constant "cash crisis."

Without a floating supply of cash, a business will experience occasional convulsions which distort, confuse, embarrass, and alarm everyone concerned with the enterprise. The owner-manager's employees and suppliers are the first to sense the nervousness of the situation. When they do, they begin to consider their futures in the light of these emergencies.

Lack of cash can drive a firm into bankruptcy even though its products are first rate and its operations are profitable.

Avoid A "Cash Crisis"

To avoid a "cash crisis" you should determine how much cash your firm needs for its normal operations. Then plan your finances to achieve the goal.

The amount of cash which a business will need differs because all businesses are not alike. Usually, for comfort, five to ten percent of a firm's working capital should be in cash.

In a sense, financial planning is what you anticipate your financial statements will show on a specific date and how you intend to get there. A cash forecast will indicate whether or not your plan of operation is feasible. A budget will indicate the availability of cash at all points of operations.

Cash Budgeting

When the subject of budgeting comes up, some owner-managers say, "That's for the big fellow. I know what my volume is and my bank account tells me how much money I have." These owners fail to realize that budgeting can help to eliminate errors of judgment made in haste or made on assumptions rather than facts.

The first thing you must know in budgeting is what your anticipated expenses are going to be for the period being budgeted. Then how much in sales must be generated to pay these expenses? What will be left? You must try to determine the high and low points in your operations in order to provide the adequate amount of cash. A sales analysis of previous periods will indicate when the high and low points occur.

This forecasting helps you to plan for financing the purchase of inventory and for carrying your accounts receivable. Controlling inventory and accounts receivable can help to take the strain off of your working capital.

Uses of a Cash Budget

The cash budget is the most effective tool for planning the cash requirements and resources of your business. With it you plan your financial operations - the cash you expect to take in and pay out. Your goal in budgeting is to maintain a satisfactory cash position for any contingency. When used to project the cash flow of the business, the cash budget will:

Provide efficient use of cash by timing cash disbursements to coincide with cash receipts. These actions may reduce the need for borrowing temporary additional working capital.

Point up cash deficiency periods so that predetermined borrowing requirements may be established and actual amounts determined to reduce excessive indebtedness.

Determine periods for repayment of borrowings.

establish the practicability of taking trade discounts or not taking them.

Determine periods of surplus cash for investment or purchase of inventory and equipment.

Indicate the adequacy or need for additional permanent working capital in the business.

Be Factual

The important thing to keep in mind in making a cash budget is the word "cash." Be as factual as you can. Try not to over-estimate sales or under-estimate expenses. Your sales forecast must be as accurate as possible because it is the basis for figuring your cash and expenses.

Use your experience to determine your cash sales. In seasonal businesses and those which have high-ticket merchandise, the percent of sales that are for cash will vary from month to month if they apply to your business.

A format such as that shown in the example below can help you to be factual. This example of a cash budget forecast uses two columns for each month. The second column allows you to insert the actual figures as they occur and helps in correcting mistakes for future forecasts.

Sound Management - Success Story

With sound management a firm can often achieve a goal by borrowing only a nominal amount. The experience of two partners in a Southeast business provides an example.

They obtained a contract to manufacture and install kitchen cabinets for a large builder. The contract called for installation in 4 months. To meet this deadline, the partners figured that they needed $56,500 in extra working capital.

Because this amount was more than they wanted to borrow, they asked for help from a counselor. The counselor helped the partners to come up with a borrowing requirement of only $16,000. This solution was arrived at by:

Arranging with their supplier to ship and bill for the materials monthly over a 3-month period.

Contracting with the builder to make an initial payment and 4 monthly payments.

Agreeing not to take any drawings from the business until the cash flow forecast indicated it was free and available.

Based on these facts, the partners estimated that during the 5 months (July through November) the firm should take in $88,000, pay out $56,500, and have a balance of $31,500 at the end of November. However, the problem was in July and August when expenses would run far ahead of the firm's income. To determine how a loan of $16,000 (including interest) could see the firm through these months, the following estimates were made:

Estimate of Borrowing Requirements To Take On Additional Contract

	July	Aug.	Sep	Oct.	Nov.
Cash Requirements					
Inventory	15,000	10,000	7,000		
Operating Expenses	4,000	6,000	6,000	4,000	2,000
Extra Equipment	2,500				
Total	**21,500**	**16,000**	**13,000**	**4,000**	**2,000**
Cash Available					
Cash on Hand	2,000			2,000	18,000
Collections	10,000	10,000	15,000	20,000	31,000
Total	**12,000**	**10,000**	**15,000**	**22,000**	**49,000**
Excess Cash Over Receipts	0	0	2,000	18,000	47,000
Additional Cash Required	9,500	6,000	0	0	0

According to these estimates, at the end of November the partners would have cash on hand amounting to $47,000. Certain obligations would be outstanding against this cash. The first one would be the repayment of the loan of $16,000. Other obligations would be those which the partners planned to accumulate during the early months of the contract when cash on hand was at a premium, such as reserve for taxes and the partners' draw.

These estimates convinced the partners that they could perform the contract if they could get a loan. The next step was to convince the bank that their plan was sound.

For the bank lending officer's benefit, as well as their own, the partners projected the loan funds through a cash flow plan for the entire business. The cash flow schedule that was prepared is shown below. It showed: (1) that the amount of money requested would be adequate for the firm's needs and (2) the margin of cash that was expected to be available both during the contract and at the end of the contract.

Keep in mind that records are a reflection of the quality of a firm's management. Nobody knows this fact better or uses it more often than a banker.

The efficiency of an owner-manager portrays itself on the profit and loss statement (income statement). The P&L of an effective operation will show adequate profits for the particular line of business. Sales, promotion, expense control, merchandise turnover, and net profit application are the points on which you will be judged.

To determine trends, the lender looks at your current financial statement and those for the past several years. The current statement also shows the lender the makeup of your net worth.

Cash Budget Forecast

	January Est.	Actual	February Est.	Actual
1. Cash in Bank (Start of Month)	1,400	1,400*	1,850	2,090*
2. Cash in Register (Start of Month)	100	100	150	70
3. Total Cash (add (1) and (2))	1,500	1,500	2,000	2,160
4. Expected Cash Sales	1,200	1,420	900	
5. Expected Collections	400	380	350	
6. Other Money Expected	100	52	50	
7. Total Receipts (add (4),(5) and (6))	1,700	1,852	1,300	
8. Total Cash and Receipts (add (3) and (7))	3,200	3,352	2,200	
9. All Disbursements (For Month)	1,200	1,192	1,000	
10. Cash Balance at End of Month in Bank Account and Register (Subtract (9) from (8))	2,000	2,160	2,300	

*The owner-manager writes in these figures as they become available.

Cash Flow Schedule - Period of Contract to Repayment of Loan

	July	Aug.	Sept.	Oct.	Nov.
Estimated Receipts					
Cash Sales	800	600	700	1,200	2,800
Accounts Receivable	10,000	10,000	15,800	20,000	31,600
Other Income	200	400	200	480	250
Total Receipts	11,000	11,200	16,700	21,680	34,650
Estimated Disbursements					
Accounts Payable	17,000	11,000	8,200	2,700	2,200
Payroll & Drawing	2,600	4,200	4,200	7,900	5,800
Expenses	1,200	1,800	2,000	2,700	600
Interest Expense	130	130	130	130	130
Plant & Equipment	2,500	460	600	800	100
Reserve for Taxes				3,800*	3,800*
Total Disbursements	23,430	17,590	15,130	18,030	12,630
Estimated Excess Receipts over Disbursements	(12,430)	(6,390)	1,570	3,650	22,020
Estimated Cash Balance at Start of Month	4,200	7,770	1,380	2,950	6,600
Borrowings	16,000				
Loan Repayment					16,000
Estimated Cash Balance at End of Month	7,770	1,380	2,950	6,600	12,620

*To be allotted in October and November so that available cash can be kept at the maximum during the months of heavy cash outflows.

Good managers recognize that occasional borrowing is one of the accepted business tools. Your long range plan for borrowing should be based on the fact that each of the various types of money in your business has its specific and appropriate purpose.

Recognizing this fact is important in preventing the misuse of fund. Keep in mind that misuse can cause a shaky financial operation. This point is especially true when operating cash seeps into long term investment in the business. As a result, the business requires a constant renewal of short term borrowings. Such borrowings indicates a capital deficiency in the business and the need for additional permanent capital.

Bear in mind that financial planning is the first step when borrowing. Such planning must be based on facts that come from your records if you are to secure loans and use them profitably.

F. Special Free Bonuses (with download instructions)

1. Doc Word Format Version of the Business Plan Template

Easily edit and modify it to meet your own specific needs (compatible with most word processors).

Copy the following link to your browser and save the file to your PC:

http://www.bizmove.com/bp/bed-and-breakfast-template.doc

2. An Extensive Generic Business Plan Template In MS Word Format

This is a high quality, full blown business plan template complete with detailed instructions and all related spread sheets. Allows you to prepare a professional business plan for any business.

Copy the following link to your browser and save the file to your PC:

http://www.bizmove.com/tools/Startup-Business-Plan-Template.doc

3. A Set of 23 Excel Spreadsheets and Tables

Use it to create the financial projections, graphs and tables required for a business plan. This includes: start-up expenses, market analysis, sales forecast, personnel plan, financial projections and more.

Copy the following link to your browser and save the file to your PC:

http://www.bizmove.com/bp/spreadseets.xls

4. Business Feasibility Study System

A complete fill in the blanks Business Feasibility Study template system. Featuring crucial things you must consider before you start pouring in your hard earned money, proven to keep you from costly mistakes when starting or expanding a business.

Copy the following link to your browser and save the file to your PC:

http://www.bizmove.com/bp/feasibility.doc

5. Business Financial Planner

This is an easy to use Excel based software program. It is a multi feature financial management program that will help you do the following:

* Plan and analyze your start up expenses and sales
* Perform Break-Even Point analysis
* Conduct 'what-if's analysis
* Perform financial ratios analysis
* Make a "go /no-go" decision
* Create financial projections

Simply type in once your business' details and assumptions and it will automatically produce a comprehensive set of financial projections and analysis for your specific business, including: Start-Up Expenses, Projected Balance Sheet, Projected Cash Flow Statement, Financial Ratios Analysis, Projected Profit and Loss Statement, Break Even Analysis, and many more.

Copy the following link to your browser and save the file to your PC:

http://www.bizmove.com/bp/projections.xlsx

Here's a detailed guide that will walk you step by step and show you exactly how to effectively use the above Business Financial Planner.

Copy the following link to your browser and save the file to your PC:

http://www.bizmove.com/bp/projections-guide.doc

6. How to Improve Your Leadership and Management Skills (eBook)

How to lead and manage people; discover powerful tips and strategies to motivate and inspire your people to bring out the best in them. Be the boss people want to give 200 percent for.

Copy the following link to your browser and save the file to your PC:

http://www.bizmove.com/bp/leadership.pdf

7. Small Business Management: Essential Ingredients for Success (eBook)

Discover scores of business management tricks, secrets and shortcuts. This program does far more than impart knowledge - it inspires action.

Copy the following link to your browser and save the file to your PC:

http://www.bizmove.com/bp/management.pdf

8. How to Create a Business Plan, Training Course (Online Video)

This training course discusses the creation of a business plan. It explains the importance of business planning defines and describes the business plan outline and its components thus enabling you to develop a very good business plan.

Copy the following link to your browser and save the file to your PC:

http://www.bizmove.com/video//business-plan-training-course.htm

9. How To Find And Attract Investors, Training Course (Online Video):

This self-paced training video will show you how to find and attract investors. Topics include determining the need for outside financing, defining what an investor is and where to find them, explaining the investment process and understanding investor expectations.

Copy the following link to your browser and save the file to your PC:

http://www.bizmove.com/business-training/how-to-find-and-attract-investors.htm

10. PowerPoint template to help create a presentation for your business plan.

Copy the following link to your browser and save the file to your PC:

www.bizmove.com/tools/Business-Plan-Presentation-Template.pptx

* * * *

36285641R00055

Printed in Great Britain
by Amazon